PRACTITIONER RESEARCH IN EDUCATION: MAKING A DIFFERENCE

D1417004

Educational Management: Research and Practice

Series Editor: Tony Bush

PRACTITIONER RESEARCH IN EDUCATION: MAKING A DIFFERENCE

David Middlewood, Marianne Coleman
and Jacky Lumby

P·C·P
Paul Chapman
Publishing Ltd

Paul Chapman Publishing Ltd
A SAGE Publications Company
6 Bonhill Street
London EC2A 4PU

SAGE Publications Inc
2455 Teller Road
Thousand Oaks, California 91320

SAGE Publications India Pvt Ltd
32, M-Block Market
Great Kailash – I
New Delhi 110 048

British Library Cataloguing in Publication Data
A catalogue record for this book is avaliable from the British Library

ISBN 1 85396 443 3
ISBN 1 85396 392 5 (pbk)

Library of Congress catalog card number available

Typeset by PDQ Typesetting, Newcastle-under-Lyme, Staffordshire.
Printed and bound in Great Britain by Athenaeum Press, Gateshead.

CONTENTS

SERIES EDITOR'S FOREWORD

Educational research has been in the spotlight in the late 1990s. This is partly because of the criticisms levelled by certain academics (Hargreaves, 1996; Tooley and Darby, 1998) and partly because of an enhanced appreciation that teaching must become a research-based profession. The Teacher Training Agency's teacher research scheme provides one modest example of an initiative to encourage teachers to research their own practice. Joyce (1991) identifies school-based research as one of the five 'doors' to school improvement. Investigating practice provides both the evidence to justify change and the probability that teachers will be motivated to innovate if they have been directly involved in identifying the need.

The introduction of self-managing schools in many countries has served to locate many more responsibilities with principals, senior staff and lay governors. While the merits and demerits of decentralisation are subject to continuing debate, there is little doubt that it gives school leaders many more levers of controls. The management of schools and other educational institutions is now largely an *internal* function and this serves to enhance the significance of school-based enquiry. Leaders who research their own practice, in schools and classrooms, are more likely to adopt policies in line with the needs of their pupils and students.

The development of effective managers in education requires the support of literature which presents the major issues in clear, intelligible language while drawing on the best of theory and research. The purpose of this series is to examine the management of schools and colleges, drawing on empirical evidence. The approach is analytical rather than descriptive and generates conclusions about the most appropriate ways of managing schools and colleges on the basis of research evidence.

The aim of this series, and of this volume, is to develop a body of literature with the following characteristics:

- Directly relevant to school and college management.
- Prepared by authors with national and international reputations.

- An analytical approach based on empirical evidence but couched in intelligible language.
- Integrating the best of theory, research and practice.

Making a Difference: the impact of practitioner research in education is the fourth volume in the series and its underlying rationale is that school-based research makes an important contribution to organisational improvement. While practitioner research is widely advocated, little is known about its effects on individuals, teams and the institution. Drawing on the extensive experience of hundreds of participants on Leicester's MBA in Educational Management, the authors show how research 'makes a difference' in a wide range of educational contexts in several countries. Linking assessment to school improvement is an essential part of the degree's philosophy, as it is in some other universities, and this book demonstrates that the approach works for many teachers and schools.

Tony Bush
University of Leicester
March 1999

PREFACE

At the turn of this century – and millennium – much debate concerns the value of current educational research. How is educational research actually perceived by the teachers and lecturers themselves? How useful and relevant is it? Who best carries it out? How is it best disseminated? Can it be free from political influence? Hegarty (1998), Director of the National Foundation for Educational Research (NFER), defines 'good' research as 'research that is relevant to the intelligence needs of teachers, trainers, administrators and policy-makers – research above all that leads to the best possible education for our children and our communities.' It is in this context perhaps that in England and Wales, the Teacher Training Agency (TTA) has stressed the need for research in schools to focus upon teaching and learning, which it deems to be most relevant to achieving high standards (TTA, 1999).

Much educational research, especially larger scale research, falls into one of two categories; either that which is commissioned by official bodies (e.g. government agencies) or that which is carried out by academic personnel, funded by authorised independent bodies (e.g. research trusts). Additionally, individuals carrying out research for doctoral theses will typically operate on a large scale. However, a widespread feature of higher education courses leading to advanced qualifications, especially Masters degrees (M.A., M.B.A., M.Ed.), is the requirement to carry out small-scale research, to be written up as assignments for the various course modules and/or final dissertations. Additionally, the TTA in England and Wales has initiated, since 1996, funding of a number of small-scale projects, encouraging individuals and schools to undertake approved research with a view to improvement and dissemination of good practice. There are, therefore, a large number of practitioners in education engaged in 'in-house' research, and reports of some of these are presented by individuals as journal articles and, occasionally, in collections of case studies, such as the various series published by the Open University as 'Readers' to accompany their Masters Degree course.

However, little is known or published about the effects of such practitioner research upon the teachers or lecturers who carry it out or upon the schools or colleges within which it occurs. This book attempts to examine this relatively unexplored area, linking its scrutiny with the context of organisational improvement. As Hopkins *et al.* (1994, p. 143) stress:

School improvement activities are frequently small-scale and focused,

and

the need to ground policy decisions in data about how the school is functioning is paramount.

(Hopkins and Lagerweij, 1996, p. 86)

School improvement, whilst inevitably and rightly focused upon improvements in learning and teaching, also relates to management at classroom, departmental and organisational levels, and the implementation of these 'policy decisions'.

The immediate stimulus for the authors of this book arises from their experience as research tutors for MBA students in Educational Management in Leicester University's Educational Management Development Unit (EMDU) based in Northampton, England. The EMDU, founded in 1992, offers a variety of routes to enable students to achieve their MBA These students are virtually all teachers or lecturers studying part-time and they can follow:

– a conventional University-based taught course, for students of the region
– a distance learning course, operating in 40 countries
– a school-based course, whereby students have tuition on their own sites, initially focused upon the Midlands region, now spread more widely across England.

The authors, therefore, had access to a very wide range of the experiences of teachers and lecturers carrying out research which had to be written up and submitted as formal assignments. The circumstances of individual students range from being a solitary teacher in a college in the United Arab Emirates, with no other colleague/teacher following the course, to being one of a group of 14 staff in one secondary school in the Midlands, all following the course and all carrying out research. Since the formal assignments are in all cases part of a course with specified content, the research is in one sense *guided*, but the student chooses the actual topic, based on considerations which include what will be of most interest and relevance to the student, the place of work or, preferably, both. It should be noted that the willingness of some schools and colleges to fund, wholly or in part, the teachers' participation in the courses led in those places to a *requirement* that the research should be directly related to issues and developments of current or future relevance to the organisation. In all cases, however, the intention of the course is to aid students in their quest for professional and institutional improvement.

The question as to the extent to which such practitioner research can 'make a difference' to the individual, the organisation or, ideally, both, needs to be set in the context of the current debate about educational research and its contribution to improvement, referred to above.

Hargreaves (1996) and Tooley and Darby (1998) have both criticised much recent and current educational research as being poor value for money and of poor quality, respectively. Bassey (1998a) has argued that the weakness lies in the failure to communicate the results of research to teachers. All these criticisms have in common the fear that current research, for whatever reason, does not appear to 'make a difference' to practice and thereby improving standards. The 'normal' practitioner, according to these criticisms, either does not know of the research, does not see it as relevant, or suspects its worth.

Yet there is widespread agreement that educational improvement – at institutional level – is based upon data systematically collected and interpreted, and that teacher involvement in this is crucial (See for example Hopkins *et al.*, 1994, p. 152 and Hopkins and Lagerweij, 1996, p. 86), because improvement ultimately occurs at institutional and indeed classroom level.

> the effectiveness of the school has to be delivered at the classroom level, and in particular in the actual teaching/learning process.
>
> (Bollen, 1996, p. 15)

There is a powerful argument for site-based research which can enlighten current practice and inform future practice in that particular place.

Hargreaves (1998, p. 47) argues that, as in medicine, 'there is rarely a single, correct treatment without alternatives', and both he and Bassey (1998) confirm that individual schools may need individual solutions. Any argument that research shows simple, unambiguous answers must be seriously challenged. As Tasker and Packham (1998) point out, research is not value-free, not even in medical science. 'A range of ideological positions' (Bassey, 1998a, p. 41) may underpin policies and practices. Although dissemination of the outcomes of research is important, Hargreaves (1998, p. 54) suggests that it is 'naive' to think this alone improves practice. Among the strategies, additional to dissemination, that he proposes are:

- More research that is relevant and teachers to do more of that research. This involvement ensures its relevance and helps teachers make better decisions about what is effective.
- Teachers become 'co-producers' of research, when 'teachers become

creators of research knowledge, the research act in itself is a fundamental form of the professional development of teachers.' (*ibid.*)

All these factors lead the authors to believe that the examination of the impact of examples of practitioner research will prove a valuable contribution to this debate.

The focus of the MBA, to which the research described in this book relates, is of course educational *management*. The premises on which the authors – and their colleagues in EMDU – base their work in this field is that the purpose of management is ultimately to support and improve practice in what is the key purpose of schools and colleges, i.e. learning and teaching. While the TTA (1999) stresses that the thrust of research must be teaching and learning, it is interesting to note that among the examples of important and approved research topics listed are, for example:

- 'the head's role in *implementing* a *system* of *monitoring* classroom practice.'
- 'how INSET and *evaluation* improve the quality of pupils' educational experience.'

The italicised words (our italics) emphasise the management aspects of the research. The authors believe that improvements in management and leadership which can arise from practitioner research offer the opportunity to contribute significantly to improvements in learning and teaching.

The book itself is divided into three sections. Following an introductory chapter, which locates practitioner research in relation to both school improvement and research paradigms, Jacky Lumby and Marianne Coleman in Section A describe and examine research undertaken by individuals in a wide variety of original contexts, all concerned with different aspects of educational management. Chapter 2 deals with investigations into staff management, and Chapter 3 examines the ways in which roles in schools or colleges can be re-assessed through research. Chapter 4 covers individuals' research into curriculum management and Chapter 5 describes and examines investigations into the structures and cultures of the organisations of individual researchers.

In Section B, David Middlewood describes work that has been done by teachers following the school-based route mentioned earlier. In those schools, where more than one teacher carried out research, the author investigates impact upon those schools as institutions. All the research here relates to schools in the Midlands area of England, because it was in that area that the courses first developed and thus where the school-based developments were sufficiently advanced for the investigations to be undertaken. Chapter 6 examines the effects of research upon staff and staff/student relationships in such schools. Chapter 7 examines three case study schools from the point of view of the extent to which the research affected their cultures. Chapter 8, more briefly, considers some examples of changes in policy and practice engendered by practitioner researchers and the extent to which management can embed such change.

In the first chapter in Section C, Marianne Coleman attempts to summarise what appear to be the conditions that offer the best opportunity for site-based research to be effective, and considers the research methods most used by practitioners. In Chapter 10 she draws some overall conclusions for such research and its management.

Different approaches and styles have been adopted as being appropriate for different sections of this book. In Section B, actual students' first names are used to give authenticity and in Chapter 7 and elsewhere the actual names of the case study schools are given. All of these are, of course, with full permission of those concerned. Elsewhere, as discussed in this book, research is sensitive for some students and it was important that their anonymity was preserved.

Just as the book offers different approaches, it is possible that its readers may wish to draw different things from it. Those who are primarily interested in how to carry out research will perhaps find their most relevant material in Chapter 1, as well as practical advice in Chapter 9. Those whose main interest lies in school improvement will find the chapters of Section B most directly relevant, as well as Chapter 10 which draws out the implications of research in schools and colleges and its particular relation to ideas of improvement. Those who wish to look for exemplification of the types of research that individuals can carry out in a school or college will find these in particular in the chapters in Section A. The editors believe all these three interests are closely related and eventually depend upon each other, but they recognise that, initially, individual readers may wish to focus upon one area.

We, the authors, are above all extremely grateful to all those teachers and lecturers who gave permission for us to use their work and for their co-operation in our research. This gratitude extends to those whose work we were, regrettably, not able to include because of space limitation. We are also very grateful to colleagues at EMDU for their interest and comments, and especially Sue Robertson for all her work on the manuscript, to Christine Wise for compiling the indices, to Marianne Lagrange at Paul Chapman Publishing for her support and of course to our families who have accepted the time we have spent on this project with more understanding than we have any right to expect.

David Middlewood
Marianne Coleman
Jacky Lumby   April 1999

THE SIGNIFICANCE OF SITE-BASED PRACTITIONER RESEARCH IN EDUCATIONAL MANAGEMENT

Marianne Coleman and Jacky Lumby

INTRODUCTION

As lecturers in educational management, supervising the work of many students carrying out small-scale research projects in their schools and colleges, we are aware of the potential that this site-based research has for school improvement. The debate about the value and quality of educational research started by Hargreaves (1996) has focused on the academic research community. Criticisms of research, particularly relating to its relevance to policy and practice, have largely been addressed to research undertaken by academics rather than practitioners. In the light of the debate on the relevance of educational research and the current emphasis on improvement, it may be particularly apposite to examine the role that an individual researcher may take in site-based research specifically on educational management, and how this research may relate to school and college improvement.

This chapter will consider the nature of practitioner research and its relationship to research paradigms including action research and critical theory, within the context of institutional improvement.

THE RELEVANCE OF SCHOOL AND COLLEGE IMPROVEMENT

Issues of improvement and effectiveness dominate much of educational policy on a national level and of educational management on an institutional level. Whilst the literature tends to relate to schools, improvement and effectiveness are equally relevant to the college sector, where there have been pressures to increase the quality of experience of student learning, the participation rates and the levels of achievement. However, this has not led to the development of a specific range of literature or to a recognition of a movement as it has in the school sector in the UK and elsewhere. In England and Wales, schools and colleges are increasingly expected to meet targets set both externally and internally, and are also subject to inspection and the publication of information about their performance. Gray (1998) claims that schools just by responding to such external pressures have been likely to improve, and as a result:

> It was not until the mid-nineties that many schools began to face up to the real challenges of school improvement and the realisation that they were in for the long haul. The pressures began to be reflected in the year on year rates of change – they quickly halved.
>
> (p. 20)

This may go some way towards explaining a preoccupation with school improvement at the end of the 1990s, but, in fact, structured efforts at school improvement have been in existence for some time. The Guidelines for Review and Internal Development in Schools (GRIDS) handbooks were used by schools in the UK in the 1980s and a definition of school improvement in the same period, adopted by the International Schools Improvement Project (ISIP) is:

> A systematic, sustained effort aimed at change in learning conditions and other related internal conditions in one or more schools, with the ultimate aim of accomplishing educational goals more effectively.
>
> (Miles and Ekholm, 1985)

Underlying the concept of school improvement are beliefs about providing the best possible education for the individual child and thereby maximising human resource potential. This may be especially true in relation to schools in developing countries. Harber and Davies identify the conditions that may be associated with effective schools in countries undergoing 'economic stringencies' (p. 4) as:

> a degree of consistency in the goals of all the participants; flexibility in organization to maximize current learning and enable lifelong adaptability and lifelong ability to learn skills; and a democratic ethos and structure,

which not only enhances such learning but prepares children for future political participation in a more sane world.

(Harber and Davies, 1997, p. 169)

School effectiveness has generally been concerned with the measurement of the degree of success of a school, particularly measures of academic success, and making links with factors that make the school effective. However, school improvement is more concerned with processes rather than outcomes and is linked with promoting change within the school. Although the changes are expected, in the long run, to lead to improved student performance, the changes in the short run may be linked to other outcomes, e.g. staff development. However, it is very likely that an effective staff development policy will be supportive of an increase in student achievement (see Middlewood, 1997, p. 186). A key feature of school improvement is the concern with process, the end point of the process may not in itself be related directly to student achievement, but will indirectly promote it.

The particular relevance of site-based research to school improvement may be that the latter is generally seen as a 'bottom up' approach, focusing on the professional experience of teachers and on changes to processes. In contrast, school effectiveness studies tend to be more 'top-down', largely being carried out by professional researchers. In addition, school improvement, with its focus on processes, tends to make use of qualitative research techniques, whilst school effectiveness research with its focus on outcomes tends to be based on quantitative research:

> It can be seen that the disciplines of school effectiveness and school improvement have been 'coming from' very different places intellectually, methodologically and theoretically.
>
> (Reynolds *et al.*, 1996, p. 144)

School improvement implies change which according to Glatter (1988) can be considered in terms:

- of scope (broad or narrow e.g. change in one curriculum area);
- of size (the relative complexity of the change from the point of view of implementation);
- of scale (the number of units and levels of the educational system that the change involves).

(Glatter, 1988, p. 125)

Thus allowing for a great range of types of school improvement. However, research undertaken by Gray (1998) has shown that schools seeking improvement often initiate change through a range of approaches:

> Teachers reported to us that their schools had been changing the ways they were run and organised, changing their attitudes and approaches to planning, changing the ways the curriculum was organised and changing the schools'

ethos or culture. Sometimes schools were moving on all four fronts at the same time, launching, in the process, a dozen or more initiatives.

(p. 22)

The link between school improvement and the leadership and culture of the institution is a strong one. If change for improvement is to occur it cannot be successful if it runs counter to the culture of the institution. Hopkins (1994, p. 77) considers that school improvement can only take place in a context where there are strategies: 'that directly address the culture of the school'. The difficulties of attempting to change the culture of the institution are considerable, but there is a range of ways in which the impetus for change may come about. These ways could include the introduction of school development planning or the appointment of a new principal. Alternatively the stimulation for change could come from outside the institution, for example an inspection, or a threat of closure. In attempting to change the culture of a school or college there may be particular links with site-based research. Joyce (1991) draws on experience in the United States to suggest five 'doors' that each open a passageway to improvement; amongst these 'doors' is listed the use of research findings by others and the collection of data about the specific institution. The five 'doors' to school improvement are suggested as:

- Collegiality: developing cohesive professional relations within schools.
- Research: helping school staff to study research findings about effective school practices or instructional alternatives.
- Site-specific information: helping staff to collect and analyse data about their schools and their students' progress.
- Curriculum initiatives: introducing changes within subject areas or across the curriculum.
- Instructional initiatives: organising teachers to study teaching skills and strategies.

Despite the identification of research as one of the 'doors' that may lead to school improvement, the debate on educational policy has raised doubts about the motivation and quality of research in education, particularly as undertaken by professional researchers. These doubts may also lead us to examine the nature of research undertaken by practitioners in schools and colleges.

QUESTIONING EDUCATIONAL RESEARCH

Gray (1998) summed up the official view of educational research at the end of the 1980s and beginning of the 1990s as: 'profound and ingrained scepticism'.

> Research was, at best, something to be annexed if it supported the cause, rubbished if it did not. It has little place in the greater scheme of things.
>
> (p.2)

In the UK, this attitude was forcibly expressed by Hargreaves (1996), who condemned educational research as not being good value for money, and as being divorced from educational practice. National reports on educational research have been no more positive. A report undertaken for OFSTED (Tooley and Darby, 1998) which has in turn been criticised on its research methodology, summarised their review of 41 published academic journal articles, picking out four themes:

- partisanship of research, expressed through its conduct and its presentation;

- methodological issues such as the absence of information about sampling and sample size, and particularly in relation to qualitative research, the lack of triangulation;

- the poor standard of some non-empirical journal articles based on the 'adulation of "great" thinkers' (p.6);

- the general (although sometimes tenuous) relevance of the research reviewed to educational policy and practice.

A further general criticism concerned dissemination of findings:

> The picture emerged of researchers doing their research largely in a vacuum, unnoticed and unheeded by anyone else.
>
> (*ibid.*, p.6)

A DfEE-commissioned report on educational research in schools (Hillage *et al.*, 1998) again mainly addressed the academic research community, seeing a need for more coherence for research through a national education research forum and improvements in the quality and dissemination of research. The report was based on the evidence of interviews with 40 stakeholders in educational research at a national level and a 'call for evidence' from the research community, local education authorities and trades unions.

The debate about the relevance of educational research and its relationship to practice is not limited to the UK. A lead article in a journal of the American Educational Research Association reviews four hypotheses: 'put forward to account for a perceived lack of connection between research and practice' (Kennedy, 1997, p. 4). As in the UK, the concerns were mainly with methodology and the relevance and accessibility of research. The involvement of teachers is seen as one way of making research more relevant.

PRACTITIONER RESEARCH

Although the national debate has centred on academic researchers who are likely to be involved in funded national research projects and in writing for the academic community, aspects of the debate have been concerned with making this research more relevant to practitioners. Hargreaves' argument for making educational research more relevant emphasised:

> the involvement of user communities, policy makers and practitioners, in all aspects of the research process, from the creation of strategic research plans, the selection of research priorities and the funding of projects through to the dissemination and implementation of policies and practices arising from or influenced by research findings.
>
> (Hargreaves, 1996, p. 6)

In the review of educational research undertaken by Hillage *et al.* (1998), there was general agreement on the involvement of teachers in the research process, but the notion of teachers-as-researchers raised two separate and contradictory views:

> One side questioned their expertise and the general value of their outputs, and the other stressed the importance of research activity as a means of accentuating teacher learning and reflective practice.
>
> (Hillage *et al.*, 1998, p. 2)

Although the OFSTED review was focused on the academic community of educational researchers the authors still commented on practitioners as researchers:

> cautious conclusions were drawn suggesting doubts about the efficacy of teachers-as-researchers to solve any of the problems noted here.
>
> (Tooley and Darby, 1998, p. 6)

There would appear to be some concerns about the ability of teachers to undertake research and about the quality of findings from such research. The doubt that is expressed about the ability of teachers to undertake research may well be felt by the teachers themselves:

> As a primary teacher in the past I have seen myself for many years as a member of an often scorned theoretical underclass. Educational theory was a commodity made by experts in other higher order institutions. It was difficult. It was exclusive. It was superior. Its creation and purpose were disconnected from earthly thoughts, practices and experiences of people like myself in schools.
>
> (Dadds, 1995, p. 2)

There may even be a political dimension to this. Wagner (1997) outlines an argument that:

traditional forms of educational research reflect asymmetries of power and knowledge that exploit, disempower, or mystify practitioner and subject populations.

(p. 13)

It may also be that the relatively practical knowledge generated by teacher research, particularly that undertaken in the classroom, is regarded as: ' "low-status" knowledge bounded by the everyday, excessively local and particular, and possibly trivial' (Cochran-Smith and Lytle, 1998). However, despite negative perceptions such as these, there are a growing number of ways in which individual teachers or groups of teachers in schools and colleges are working in partnership with colleagues in higher education, or in other ways acting as teacher-as-researcher.

WHAT IS PRACTITIONER RESEARCH?

Practitioners in schools and colleges are teachers and lecturers, but also those who might be considered as professionals in education, for example administrators, managers and librarians.

The definition of research offered by Johnson (1994) is:

A focused and systematic enquiry that goes beyond generally available knowledge to acquire specialised and detailed information, providing a basis for analysis and elucidatory comment on the topic of enquiry.

(Johnson, 1994, p. 3)

Research of this type may be undertaken within the context of a course such as the Leicester MBA in Educational Management and other similar master's level courses. Alternatively, it may be undertaken in the cause of professional development as in the training for the National Professional Qualification for Headteachers (NPQH), or as part of a school- or college-based investigation initiated within the institution or by an external partner. The Teacher Training Agency (TTA) has sponsored teacher research projects in schools in England and Wales with external partners involved in the research.

Linking practitioner research to school improvement and to professional development, within the context of the teacher working towards accreditation, indicates the complex nature of the role of the teacher-researcher:

The multiple challenges to be overcome by the teacher-researcher as she seeks to extend her learning for her own benefit through empirical enquiry; as she seeks to please the academy's tutors and examiners in construction of her written texts; as she seeks to reflect upon and develop her practical professional work for her pupils' sakes; and as she seeks to contribute some of her professional learning to her colleagues' development and the healthy growth of her workplace. She has these several audiences and these several purposes, with the concomitant task of trying to reconcile them all in the same teacher research process.

(Dadds, 1995, p. 111)

Summing up the position in the United States, Cochran-Smith and Lytle (1998) identify teacher research; as it is linked to programmes of professional development; as it is linked to re-structuring and organisational change and as it may be linked towards movements for social change and justice:

> In each of these efforts, the concept of teacher research carries with it an enlarged view of the teacher's role – as decision maker, consultant, curriculum developer, analyst, activist, school leader – as well as enhanced understandings of the contexts of educational change.
>
> (Cochran-Smith and Lytle, 1998, p. 20)

Carter and Halsall (1998, pp. 73–4) identify practitioner research primarily as working towards school improvement and see the characteristics of teacher research as:

> grounded in data which has been systematically collected and analysed for a clearly defined purpose;
>
> undertaken by teachers, though sometimes with the support of external critical friends;
>
> it focuses on professional activity, usually in the workplace itself;
>
> its purpose is to clarify aspects of that activity, with a view to bringing about beneficial change – ultimately, to improve student progress, achievement and development, this being precisely the purpose of school improvement itself;
>
> it may focus on, again as is the case with school improvement efforts generally, both teaching and learning at the classroom level, and supporting organisational conditions and change management capacity.

Not all practitioner research is undertaken by practitioners alone, the presence of an external partner may be required as a prerequisite of the research, or may be entered into as a natural process arising from the partnership between higher education institutions and schools (see Middlewood and Parker, 1998). Wagner (1997) points out that teachers have always contributed to educational research, at least as subjects of the research, in this they may have entered a 'data extraction agreement' (p. 15), but researchers, in the effort to make educational research more relevant, have tended to involve teachers in other ways. He terms co-operation between a researcher and a practitioner 'clinical partnership', but also outlines a further model 'co-learning agreement'. This relationship may be exemplified by feminist research where the researcher does not maintain a distance but seeks involvement leading to mutual learning and understanding. Strachan (1993) researching women in educational leadership reported on research that had elements of co-learning. Her research was:

> full of the 'personal' and the 'subjective'. The research process was not very orderly or, at times, very coherent. I was, however, 'inside' the culture and participating in the process (Oakley, 1981). This 'personal involvement' was not a dangerous bias but a necessary prerequisite condition of the sharing of intimate information.
>
> (p. 76)

The forms of co-operation between the practitioner and the external researcher are shown in Table 1.1.

Table 1.1 *Inquiry roles of researchers and practitioners within different forms of co-operative educational research*

Inquiry Role	Data Extraction Agreement	Clinical Partnership	Co-learning Agreement
Object of inquiry	Practitioners	Practitioners	Practitioners Researchers
Agent of inquiry	Researchers	Researchers Practitioners	Researchers Practitioners

A practitioner researcher may undertake research as an individual, with others in the school or college or with an external partner who may be a professional researcher. In order to consider the significance of site-based research it may be helpful to consider the processes and possible purposes of the research in terms of the basic conceptual thinking or paradigms that underlay it.

RESEARCH PARADIGMS AND THEIR RELATIONSHIP TO PRACTITIONER RESEARCH

Paradigms may be defined as:

> frameworks that function as maps or guides for scientific communities, determining important problems or issues for its members to address and defining acceptable theories or explanations, methods and techniques to solve defined problems.
>
> (Usher, 1996, p. 15)

A paradigm shift may occur when a dominant paradigm is overthrown and a new paradigm takes its place. Such a shift involves a new way of looking at the world.

The Positivist and Interpretive Paradigms

These are the two basic research paradigms that act as frameworks for researchers, one is the positivist paradigm, the other the interpretive paradigm.

In the positivist approach quantitative methods are likely to be used. Positivist methodology is based on the use of the scientific method and, at its most extreme, seeks to 'discover' general laws explaining the nature of the reality that the researcher is observing and recording.

The key idea of positivism is that the researched world exists externally and aspects of it can be measured through objective methods. 'Knowledge is only of significance if it is based on observations of this external reality' (Easterby-Smith *et al.*, 1994, p. 77).

In positivist thinking, a social reality exists and it is possible through empirical research to establish sets of social 'facts'. There is likely to be an attempt to identify causality. The implications are that the observer is independent of what is observed and that the research is value free.

The other paradigm is generally known as interpretive, but may also be called relativist or phenomenological. This approach is likely to be used where complex issues are involved, e.g. in research where the interplay of social, cultural and political factors has meant that methods such as life history, interview and observation have been judged the most appropriate methods of research. The stress has been on the subjective reality for individuals. In this approach:

> The principal concern is with an understanding of the way in which the individual creates, modifies and interprets the world in which he or she finds himself or herself.
>
> (Cohen and Manion, 1994, p. 8)

Through a variety of qualitative methods it is considered possible to build up a picture of a social 'reality'. Such a view is opposed to a strictly positivist view, which is more often associated with purely quantitative methods. In interpretive research:

> the task of the social scientist should not be to gather facts and measure how often certain patterns occur, but to appreciate the different constructions and meanings that people place upon their experience.
>
> (Easterby-Smith *et al.*, 1994, p. 78)

The subject is involved in the research in a way that could not occur within the positivist paradigm. Bogden and Biklen (1992, p. 24) describe an 'empathic' perspective; that is they call for sympathy and under-standing towards those whom they study. This interpretive approach stresses that it is the subjective experience of the individual that is important and that it is individual perception that bestows meaning, rather than there being any external objective meaning. This stems from the view that:

> the world and 'reality' are not objective and exterior, but that they are socially constructed and given meaning by people.
>
> (Easterby-Smith, et al., 1994, p. 78)

People act on the basis of the sense that they individually make of a situation, rather than acting directly in response to external stimuli. It is assumed that all human action is meaningful:

> and hence has to be interpreted and understood within the context of social practices.
>
> (Usher, 1996, p. 18)

Key features of positivist and interpretive paradigms are shown in Table 1.2:

Table 1.2   Features of positivist and interpretive paradigms

Positivist	*Interpretive*
The world is external and objective	The world is socially constructed and subjective
The observer is independent	The observer is part of what is observed
Science is value free	Science is driven by human interests
The focus is on facts	The focus is on meanings
Search for causality	Try to understand what is happening
Reduce to simplest elements	Look at the totality of the situation
Formulating concepts for measurement	Using multiple methods to establish different views of the phenomena
Large samples	Small samples looked at in depth or over time.

(adapted from Easterby-Smith, 1994, p. 80)

There is an obvious connection between the gathering of quantitative data and a positivist approach, and qualitative data and a relativist or interpretive approach.

Statement of the two extreme approaches masks the fact that, in practice, the approaches need not be mutually exclusive and are often used together. In practice, research may encompass elements of the two apparently opposed paradigms. Cohen and Manion (1994) refer to systematic, scientific research that considers 'people within their social contexts' (p. 40). Miles and Huberman (1994) comment on the difficulty of finding working researchers in a fixed position on the spectrum:

> we believe that all of us – realists, intepretivists, critical theorists – are closer to the center, with multiple overlaps.
>
> (p. 5)

> a growing body of social research takes a stand somewhere between the two schools of thought. It is recognised that no piece of social research can be entirely objective, since no researcher is value free. Even in an overtly rigorous quantitative, head-counting study, some implicit decisions have already been made as to which heads are worth counting.
>
> (Johnson, 1994, p. 7)

Researchers may adopt a flexible approach to the gathering of data, complementing a questionnaire with a more in-depth qualitative research approach. For example, the combination of a postal questionnaire with detailed interviews might provide an opportunity of obtaining a large amount of quantitative data, as well as rich qualitative data. However, the combination of the two approaches raises the question of the relative significance of the underlying research methodologies in any research project.

In our experience the practitioner researcher is likely to make use of both qualitative and quantitative techniques thus adopting a stance, knowingly or unknowingly, that incorporates some elements from both of the two basic paradigms.

PARADIGMS RELATING TO THE PURPOSE OF PRACTITIONER RESEARCH

1 Critical Theory

Habermas (1972) argues that both the different research traditions of positivism and relativism or interpretivism are linked with particular social interests. Neither of these is therefore likely to inspire research that brings about freedom, justice and democracy.

A third type of research tradition, critical theory, is emancipatory, a critique of ideology, implying the taking of action to change situations. In this theory there can be no 'objective' knowledge since every view is influenced by a social interest. Feminist methodology relates to critical theory since it implies a commitment to change. Feminist research is likely to contain an overtly political agenda. Adler *et al.* (1993) considered feminist research as: 'essentially political, concerned not only with exposure but also with change' (p. 57). Within this paradigm of critical theory, it is possible to use a range of positivist and interpretive approaches. What is important is that the research that is done will be informed by the feminist scholarship of the researchers.

> feminism is about putting women first – about judging their interests to be important and insufficiently represented within mainstream politics and the academic world.

> (Purvis, 1985, p. 80)

However, positivist methodology may be seen as restrictive in feminist research:

> Positivist methods, such as questionnaires, that generate reproducible and generalisable results are viewed as 'truths' yet they do not allow women to express their own attitudes in their own words or allow them greater power in setting the research agenda.

> (Verma, 1998, p. 38)

In this case, the practitioner researcher went on to justify her choice of research tool:

> Thus feminist methodology favouring qualitative methods best suits the aims of my research. Although there are many issues within this approach, how individual women teachers construct their own identities and understand themselves in both their personal and professional lives means that in-depth interviews are essential to the way I research career patterns.

> (*ibid.*)

Cochran-Smith and Lytle (1998, p. 29) consider that feminist research and teacher research have much in common:

> teacher researchers (like feminists) actually use familiar research methods in new ways as they struggle to construct research that is designed to be *for* teachers and learners and not simply *about* them.

2 Action Research

Elliott (1991) is a key figure in the development of action research. He sums up the nature of action research thus:

the fundamental aim of action research is to improve practice rather than to produce knowledge.

(Elliott, 1991, p. 49)

In the improvement of practice, there are seen to be two aspects of action research: one is to bring about change, the other to promote reflection among practitioners. The concepts of the 'reflective practitioner', or of 'reflection in action' are associated with Schön (1984), who sees reflection in action as:

reflection, in a context of action, on phenomena which are perceived as incongruent with intuitive understandings.

Or,

a reflective conversation with the situation.

(p. 42)

An important aspect of action research is therefore the potential that there is for the practitioner researcher to elucidate their understanding of processes in education and to enhance their own learning:

There was evidence from the teacher questionnaires and interviews of other learning beyond that formally expressed in the research reports. There was evidence of perceptual and attitudinal changes generated by the research that caused teachers to think, perceive and feel anew.

(Dadds, 1995, p. 112)

However, the two aspects of action research, the promotion of change, and the concept of reflection in action are allied, with perhaps 'action' being the key word:

This implies that action research does not have to be something carried out by a special group of people called researchers but is in fact what any practitioner could do as part of everyday practice, given certain conditions. Reflective practitioners are *ipso facto* researchers into their own practice.

(Bryant, 1996, p. 115)

Action research can be seen as a spiral. It is a process that views action following evaluation or reflection as part of one cyclical process to be followed by another. This involvement with the processes of education while they are taking place is a dynamic involvement rather than a passive observation.

Although action research does make use of empirical methods, Johnson (1994) criticises the approach from a positivist stance, since action research generally involves trying to change/improve the situation that is being audited and monitored through the use of research methods. The intention to change the situation whilst researching it is antipathetic to a purely positivist view that the researcher should stand outside the research situation and remain objective. However, there is much in practitioner research leading to school improvement that is close to action

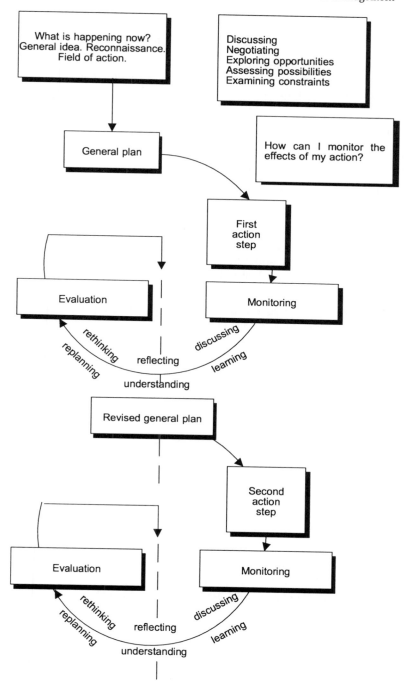

Figure 1.1 The Action Research Spiral (adapted from Marsh, 1992, p. 119)

research.

Ebbutt defines action research as involving:

> the systematic study of attempts to change and improve educational practice
> by groups of participants by means of their own practical actions and by
> means of their own reflection upon the effects of those actions.
>
> (Ebbutt, 1985, p. 156 quoted in Bryant, 1996, p. 114)

This emphasises several points that are relevant to the subject of this book:

1. the role of practitioners
2. the importance of improving practice
3. the importance of reflection upon the effects of action.

Bassey (1998) helpfully sets out eight stages of action research which
clearly show how the change becomes *part* of the action research process.

Stage 1: Define the inquiry
What is the issue of concern? What research question are we asking? Who will
be involved? Where and when will it happen?

Stage 2: Describe the educational situation
What are we required to do here? What are we trying to do here? What
thinking underpins what we are doing?

Stage 3: Collect evaluative data and analyse it
What is happening in this educational situation now as understood by the
various participants? Using research methods, what can we find out about it?

Stage 4: Review the data and look for contradictions
What contradictions are there between what we would like to happen and
what seems to happen?

Stage 5: Tackle a contradiction by introducing change
By reflecting critically and creatively on the contradictions what change can
we introduce which we think is likely to be beneficial?

Stage 6: Monitor the change
What happens day-by-day when the change is introduced?

Stage 7: Analyse evaluative data about the change
What is happening in this educational situation now – as understood by the
various participants – as a result of the changes introduced? Using research
methods what can we find out about it?

Stage 8: Review the change and decide what to do next
Was the change worthwhile? Are we going to continue it in the future? What
are we going to do next? Is the change sufficient?

(Bassey, 1998b, pp. 94–5)

In this sequence, the point where action research deviates from a positivist
approach is at Stage 5, when the researcher deliberately introduces change
to the observed situation and then monitors the effect:

Unlike some other forms of research, action research is not seeking objective descriptions of the *status quo*, it is using research methods to initiate worthwhile change.

(Bassey, 1998b, p. 108)

In this, action research may be seen to relate to critical theory with its commitment to change:

Increasingly, teacher research and related approaches to practitioner inquiry, especially action research, are positioned as vehicles for radical critique and challenge, designed explicitly to interrogate and alter the arrangements of schooling that perpetuate systemic inequities.

(Cochran-Smith and Lytle, 1998, p. 20)

Thus, action research becomes more important as a vehicle for change rather than being simply a means of investigation. In this case (Dadds, 1995) points out that the action researcher needs an understanding of the nature of change:

Without some working and workable personal theory of change, application of research into classrooms or institutional practice may be a hazardous affair.

(Dadds, 1995, p. 142)

The researcher may also need the micro-political skills that allow them to make judgements about particular circumstances relating to change, and about the people involved in change so that: 'theories and insights can be used to improve their corner of the world.' (*ibid.*)

The notion of the use of action research for change and for the researcher to have an understanding of the change process necessitates a decision about what change is worthwhile, a normative decision that would not sit within the framework of the tradition of positivist research:

Thus for the action researcher the question is not simply about how practice can be improved, but also whether the practice is worth improving.

(Dadds, 1995, p. 137)

Locke (1990, p. 202) refers to 'making a better world' through the use of research, but stresses that the research itself should be rigorous, so that our knowledge and understanding is: 'based on sound evidence, tested theory and workable philosophy.' This thinking is very much in accord with a view of research in education in the developing world, where it is advocated:

that school organization and management must look beyond the bureaucratic present to more democratic forms of school management that can ease the burden of [such] problems, enhance the internal search for solutions and coping mechanisms and improve school effectiveness/decrease school ineffectiveness.

(Harber and Davies, 1998, p. 151)

The next four chapters focus on the experience of the sole practitioner researcher as he or she researches particular aspects of the management of their organisation. In each case the intention of the researcher was to achieve an improvement ultimately on the teaching and learning of students, sometimes directly, through a focus on the management of the curriculum, sometimes indirectly, through addressing issues of the management of structures or of people. As Dadds points out:

> There is a long tradition supporting the concept of action oriented approaches to research. In this tradition, small groups and communities across the globe have sought, in various ways, to change their circumstances and lives. Knowledge and understanding generated by the enquiry process have been the foundation of action.
>
> (Dadds, 1995, p. 135)

Cochran-Smith & Lytle (1998) argue that practitioner researchers use research in a distinctive way, drawing parallels with feminist research approaches. They argue that teacher researchers 'struggle to construct research that is designed to be for teachers and learners and not simply about them', and in so doing, exploit:

> the potential of research that is intentionally political and intentionally attentive to the perspectives of insiders committed to improving the life chances of schoolchildren, schoolteachers, and the families and communities they serve.
>
> (Cochran-Smith and Lytle, 1998, p. 29)

As Locke (1990, p. 202) asserts, this does not mean that the research can consequently be less rigorous. The desire to make 'a better world' is predicated on the imperative to be 'as right and truthful as possible'. What differs is not the care with which research is designed and implemented, but the driving force to reach an end point of change in the school or college.

Change can be seen as impacting on the individual researcher and/or on the organisation. Disentangling the two can be difficult and misleading. Huberman (1993, pp. 41–43) distinguishes 'instrumental effects' which are 'changes in tools or methods of daily work; changes in policies or practices at a more institutional level' and 'conceptual effects' which are 'clear conceptual connections between the main findings of the study and the informants' work situation'. The former would seem to indicate the research impacting at an organisational level, the latter impacting on the individual. However, change works through individuals who adjust their thinking and practice. Such changes in conceptual understanding and attitude may precede changes in practice, and influence action over many years. From a reverse perspective, changes in practice may influence conceptual understanding and attitudes over time. In attempting to assess the impact of research, a pragmatic differentiation can be made of how far conceptual thinking was influenced in the individual researcher and in others, and how far practice changed, but the perspective is a snapshot at one point in time which assesses impact so far, and which is consequently partial and imperfect, and neatly disentangles those aspects which may be messily conflated in practice.

In summary, there may be a number of potential paradoxes in practitioner research. The impact on the individual and on the organisation can be evaluated as different and separate phenomena, and yet they are akin and symbiotic. The desire to be both rigorously objective and to incorporate micro-political awareness challenges 'scientific' approaches to research. Cochran-Smith and Lytle (1998) believe that practitioner research amounts to 'a new paradigm that aims to frontally transform rather than describe a school or classroom setting' (*op. cit.*, p. 31). The following chapters will examine, through examples of practitioner researchers in action, why they embarked on research, what they hoped to gain for themselves and their organisation, why they chose the methods they did, what promoted or inhibited the research having an impact, and finally, what they feel were the results of the work that they had undertaken. In attempting to answer these questions, the apparent paradoxes and the possibility for 'a new paradigm' will be explored.

SECTION A:
DEVELOPING ASPECTS
OF MANAGEMENT

2

DEVELOPING THE MANAGEMENT OF PEOPLE

Jacky Lumby

INTRODUCTION

It all boils down to one thing: people, people, people, people. I don't care what country, or what organization, or what team you are in – it is the people and whether you can organize those people to achieve an end result that count ...
(Morgan, 1989, p. 33)

These words set the context for the management of people in schools and colleges. The twin themes of the critical importance of people and the changing environment in which those people work are well rehearsed (Wagstaff, 1994; O'Neill, 1994b; Bush, 1997). In schools in the UK, the routes into teaching have expanded. There are shortages in subject areas and management roles. The distinction between teaching and associate staff has blurred. In colleges, almost half the work force are part-time (FEDA, 1995) and the demise of a national pay and reward system has led to a variety of working conditions. Throughout the world, teachers and educational managers experience high stress levels (Travers and Cooper, 1996; Earley, 1994; Punch and Tuettmann, 1990; Chan and Hui, 1995). The effective management of educational staff has never been more challenging.

The means adopted to achieve such effective management have been both technical and transformational. The technical means have involved the development of human resource management systems, for example, more sophisticated recruitment and selection procedures, complex pay and reward policies, the monitoring of staff performance and outcomes. Transformational approaches adopt a more radical approach, arguing that while technical developments may be helpful, they will not be sufficient to equip staff or their organisations to transcend discontinuous change (Lumby, 1997). A more fundamental change process may be needed, for example using the concept and practice of a learning organisation. The latter assumes a leadership role which is primarily to manage learning:

> The new view of leadership in learning organizations centers on subtler and more important tasks. In a learning organization, leaders are designers, stewards, and teachers. They are responsible for building organizations where people continually expand their capabilities to understand complexity, clarify vision, and improve shared mental models – that is, they are responsible for learning.
>
> (Senge, 1990, p. 340)

Garratt describes the conditions which would prevail in an organisation where learning is central:

1. People at all levels of the organization are encouraged to learn regularly and rigorously from their work and to feed back such learning to other parts of the organization which could use them

2. Systems are set up to ensure that the learning is moved to those parts of the organization which need it

3. Learning is valued and rewarded in the organization

4. The organization is seen to continuously transform itself through the application of its learning, led by the attitudes and behaviours of its directors.

> (Garratt, 1994, p. 59)

What is implied is that learning and its dissemination is systematic. The potential contribution of practitioner research appears to be very much in line with thinking on how a learning organisation can be achieved. Practitioner research supports the process of learning as it is sustained and systematic, and provides a vehicle for organisational learning through sharing with others the resulting lessons and recommendations.

This chapter focuses on how practitioner research can contribute to the effective management of people using three case examples to examine whether the learning which results is in fact individual or organisational learning. The first two examples explore research on the induction of staff in a primary and a secondary school. The final example concerns a college-wide survey assessing staff motivation and morale. In each case the research undertaken may lead to a growth of conceptual under-standing in the individual. To meet the criteria for achieving a learning organisation, it must also achieve conceptual and instrumental change in others on a sufficient scale to effect organisational systems.

MENTORING STAFF

The first UK example focuses on the research of the head of Sixth Form at a secondary school in the East of England. Shortly after completing the research he was made redundant. The focus of the research was the induction and mentoring of new staff. Interest in this area was long-standing, stemming from the time he was involved in TVEI in the early 1990s. Undertaking an MBA with Leicester University gave him an opportunity to pursue that interest. He felt that although some work on induction had taken place in schools, there was still a lot of uncertainty about the purpose of induction and mentoring, that it was usually limited to teachers and did not include other staff, and that it focused on the socialisation aspects of the process:

> I firmly believe that it should be much more than that. There is scope for some really exciting developments.

A postal survey of a random selection of schools in the South and Midlands of England provided data on the induction and mentoring policy and practice of nine schools. It appeared that there was 'fragmentation of planning, development and implementation' and much variation in the quality. Throughout the research a number of ideas were suggested as to how induction and mentoring could be conceptualised and put into operation to achieve not only social transition for newly qualified staff, but also a professional effectiveness focus for all staff new to a post or to a school. The work was undertaken as an individual project, as senior management had previously expressed little interest. The researcher and the member of staff responsible for induction in the school were interviewed to assess how far the research had had an impact.

The anticipated personal outcomes were achieved. The researcher had felt isolated in his views and was reassured through his reading that his ideas on what induction and mentoring could be and could achieve were not those of a lone voice but were very much supported by previous research. The process was therefore enjoyable and confidence building, but also led to frustration in wondering how the results of the research could be used to improve the practice of schools. His redundancy made further personal work in his school impossible. However the research was sent to the member of staff responsible for induction. She read it and used many of the suggestions:

> It did alter my perspective on mentoring and I did use ... some ideas that I had gleaned from it, to make my induction programme more useful. I felt that perhaps I had not seen the full force of what mentoring was ... I think it made me see that it could be used as more of a professional tool to help young

teachers and that I could make it more structured along a professional line ... I devised a much more structured induction programme using some of the ideas that he suggested ... I've actually involved other people in the school, more senior teachers in the school as well.

Clearly, there have been results in the school at both a conceptual and instrumental level. The researcher was also concerned to try to use the work to achieve an impact more widely and attempted to offer school development programmes on induction and mentoring. This met with little success. His belief was that schools are more focused on curriculum developments such as the national curriculum and GNVQ and see induction and mentoring as 'peripheral areas'. He felt there might even be a more fundamental barrier in that teachers may reject ideas, asking 'how is it going to impact in the classroom? This is just a management strategy which will have no impact on my day-to-day classroom activity.' If this criterion of immediate visible impact on classroom practice is applied, then many possible important developments which will have a more long-term and indirect impact on teaching and learning may be lost. The potential result of this piece of research was to focus the management process of induction more on professional practice, but because it was not directly considering a strategy for teaching and learning it may have been seen as less relevant.

There is certainly a debate on the usefulness of educational management research and on educational research generally, with detractors insisting on results which are reflected in teaching and learning. Practitioner researchers would agree that a benefit for learners must be the ultimate aim, but to suggest that research is limited to what might be referred to as first level, that is, research on what happens in the classroom itself, excluding second level, that is, practice which creates structures and support for what happens in the classroom, risks impoverished development.

INDUCTION OF NEWLY QUALIFIED TEACHERS

The potential connection between research on induction and classroom practice is demonstrated by the case example of Kents Hill First School. The researcher in this case was a deputy head who subsequently achieved her first headship at Kents Hill School. Both the headteacher and the one newly qualified teacher (NQT) appointed to the school to date were interviewed.

The Headteacher had begun her MBA while at her previous school and had worked closely with her then head to ensure that the research she did was in line with school development needs and that the recommendations were implemented. The interest in induction arose particularly because of events in the newly opened school. The experienced teachers were given larger classes than the NQT, as one means of supporting the latter. During the course of the year, the success of the school led to a large number of new pupils, many of them disaffected. The school doubled in size in one term. There was no space for the new children except in the NQT's class which consequently reached the same size as those of the experienced staff but had a disproportionate number of children who had very challenging needs. Not surprisingly, this put strains on the NQT and led to the researcher feeling it would be useful to review the whole area of the induction of NQTs.

This experience and the results of the research changed the views of the researcher, leading her to feel that the prevailing attitude to NQTs, that they are likely to save on salary costs, was misguided. She felt that the resources that had been needed to support the NQT in the situation described above could have paid for a much more experienced teacher. The time needed was also very difficult to find. As a result:

> I really do firmly believe, particularly after doing the research, that newly qualified teachers aren't a cheap option. I thought if I could highlight the fact that they aren't a cheap option, then maybe the provision for those NQTs, who are our future would be better all round for everybody. Particularly with Local Management of Schools it was 'Get a cheap teacher and you have solved your finance situation' and it really just wasn't like that ... What I really wanted to do was to highlight the fact that newly qualified teachers had a right to have the best possible start and just because they have finished their training it didn't mean that they had finished their development. There was an enormous amount that needed to carry on.

This commitment to the right of an NQT to receive professional support influenced her views on the appropriateness of recruiting NQTs. When she achieved her first headship in the newly opened Kents Hill School, only one NQT was appointed, and with some caution, giving due recognition to the support that would be needed. The selection proved a happy one, the head being well satisfied that the school had recruited a talented and efficient teacher.

The first impact of the research was the indirect role it played in the school recruiting a good teacher. Immediately after the pool interview in discussion with the NQT, the head 'talked about her commitment to NQTs and mentioned she had done this research'. The NQT visited a number of other schools and eventually accepted the post in Kents Hill. The research had played a part in this. The NQT explained:

> It was just nice to know that the Head said she had done this work and was interested in NQTs. Oh gosh! Someone's interested in me and what I'm

coming to the school with, not that they're just having an NQT because it's nice to have a young person or whatever. Just knowing these things, that I was going to get release time, that I was going to be supported, that definitely had an impact.

The NQT was given a mentor and a half-day release a week as part of her induction support. Unfortunately, maternity leave meant that she had to change mentors twice, but nevertheless, the mentoring support was continued. The half-day release was provided by the head herself covering, at some personal cost:

I was her release teacher and that was hard. It was so tempting, so tempting to sometimes say, as she was good, she was excellent, to say 'I'm so sorry I can't do it this week.' I always did my utmost to give her that.

The NQT really valued the mentoring support and the half-day release:

You can't describe it really. Brilliant. The catching up and the taking stock, things like when it's report writing time, it was just so valuable. I think I spent two of my afternoons just catching up on the paperwork, so it was useful in those respects. I also initially spent time just wandering around and looking in the resource cupboards and seeing what was where in the school and what we'd got, which you don't get to know otherwise. And then also I observed other teachers as well. We used my competency file and it was things in that that we looked at, which I felt needed to be developed or I wanted support on. You've got so much still to learn and take on board. I mean, I'm not saying that now I don't have a tremendous amount to learn, but so much is just so new. In the first few weeks it's like you're in a sort of fairytale land.

The research worked through changing the attitude, commitment and practice of the head. The result was a contribution to recruiting a good new teacher, making her feel a supported and valued member of the school and launching her professional career with an emphasis on reflection and development of classroom practice. Of course, the success of the NQT was mainly due to her personal skills and attitudes, but the induction process ensured the early best use of her talents. It also provided a safety net, in that there was never a situation in which the NQT would not perform to a satisfactory standard because the support was always there.

The Headteacher was in an ideal position to implement her research as the senior manager of the school. The results were felt in a very personal way both in her confidence and certainty in the systems she set up and in the impact on the first year of a new teacher. The research has led to the start of not just a job, but a career. As the NQT explained:

Do I see what she studied infiltrating through? Yes I think so ... I'm sure it was just more in her mind that I did need support rather than thinking of me as someone who was just cheap and that we could tuck away in there. It was not only support. I needed to be developed as well. During the latter part of the last term it was difficult with OFSTED but certainly since it's been very much 'What do you want to do with your career? How do you want to develop', which is excellent. Not many schools will pay attention to you, what you want to do.

Both the teacher and the school have benefited, and ultimately, the children and their parents.

MOTIVATING STAFF

The researcher at the Tertiary College was Principal Manager, Learning Services, (Resources). He felt some concern at the way that changes in further education since incorporation in 1993 had affected the staff, particularly their motivation, and set out to investigate his concerns. The team of middle managers was involved in the research. Consequently both the researcher and the Principal Manager, Learning Services, (Learner Support and Health Studies), a member of the middle management team, were interviewed to explore what had been achieved through the research.

The researcher had hoped to help the organisation develop its awareness of how staff felt and thought concerning their roles, responsibilities and the conditions of their work. He aimed to produce a formal statement which would be credible in assessing motivation. So much investigation is undertaken in colleges to produce data concerning the curriculum and finance for the FEFC and for planning. He felt it was important the research was not reactive to external demands as is so often the case, but proactive, because of the real concern of a member of staff. He wanted to undertake some research which centred on staff and could inform both middle and senior management of the current state of morale. He also believed that 'by giving staff a voice ... this would make them feel recognised, even if it was simply because someone had asked them the questions.' The Principal Manager, Learner Support also suspected that there had been a decline in motivation and felt that the research might provide useful information for the whole middle management team. The ultimate aim was to 'change and inform our practice'.

A survey of all full-time staff was undertaken with the active involvement of the middle management team who had some input into the design of the questionnaire and helped to distribute it with a personal explanation. The support from staff was also good, with a nearly 90 per cent return. The resulting analysis confirmed that there were factors which were having a negative impact on motivation. Staff felt that they were being asked to undertake tasks and roles for which they had not been adequately trained, that the degree of administrative support was not adequate and that there was insufficient recognition of their work, particularly from senior managers.

One difficulty that emerged was that some of the issues that were causing demotivation related more strongly to the attitudes and actions of senior rather than middle managers. The researcher recognised that this result could have been anticipated, given the greater distance that exists between lecturers and those at the top of the hierarchy, and those at middle management level. Nevertheless some of the findings were contentious and sensitive.

The middle management team discussed the resulting report and the paper has also gone to senior management for consideration. At this point in the process, the researcher was appointed to a post in another college, which has prevented his personal follow-up over the period of time that had been anticipated. Nevertheless, the work is seen as having had an impact.

The research did not lead independently to direct change. However, the findings did inform ongoing debate and as such contributed to the change process. In this case, the actual nature of the research, the figures produced, provided justification for actions which had been considered. The Principal Manager, Learner Support felt that whereas previously she might have suggested action to senior managers, her suggestions were supported only by her own perceptions.

> What has actually been achieved is to get percentages on the issues that we were in some way aware of. In terms of the perception of the culture, I would have been aware of what people perceived, but I couldn't have demonstrated it statistically.

Her belief is that the research would be translated into an action plan, and that it would be the basis of future action, despite the departure of the researcher:

> You can hardly bury it can you, because it contains some quite important information.

She also believed that the survey itself may have achieved some change:

> Once you've raised a question, then it hangs in people's minds and they think 'Now what can we do about it?' Because you've raised awareness you have then improved motivation. Any change is a change for the better, and any focus is a focus for the better. It's the Hawthorne effect ... So inevitably there will be an improvement from that very early stage.

The Hawthorne effect referred to is a seminal 1927 experiment which concluded that any expression of concern for people's welfare was in itself a motivating factor (Mayo, 1933). Certainly the research appears to have provoked discussion and greater awareness amongst staff. The return rate on questionnaires confirms the researcher's view that staff appreciated the opportunity to comment on their motivation, and to his surprise led to him gaining 'kudos with the staff for asking how they felt'.

The research made an impact on several levels. The actual process of implementing the investigation in itself may have influenced the motivation of staff and the personal standing of the researcher. The middle management team has acquired data which can be used to give impetus to addressing concerns which had been felt and plans which had been in place, but gained from the additional relevant evidence. At the organisational level, the research is in the process of being considered formally by middle and senior managers and seems likely to lead to at least some action. There is as yet no evidence that the more sensitive issues centring on the relationship between staff and senior management will be addressed, and this may relate to the context in which the research was undertaken. The researcher felt that for research to have the greatest impact:

> the recommendations would have to have been commissioned by the people who need to make the changes or [that] they would have had to have been involved in it themselves.

There was some involvement from senior managers at the inception of the research, but perhaps insufficient to lay the foundations for considering the organisation-wide cultural issues which arose. Research undertaken by middle managers which results in criticism of the actions of senior managers is a difficult issue, and again highlights that the potential impact of research relies critically on micropolitical skills. Despite the unresolved cultural issues which resulted from this piece of work, it has nevertheless been felt in the personal lives of staff and the researcher and offered a means of promoting action. As the researcher put it, the real basis for action was that now 'we understand ourselves better'.

THE IMPACT OF RESEARCH ON MANAGING PEOPLE

The Headteacher at Kents Hill School noted that being Headteacher meant you were in an ideal position to implement the results of research. For practitioner researchers in less senior positions, accessing sufficient support at a senior level may be critical to fully utilising what has been learned through research. This chapter commenced by suggesting that in a rapidly changing environment, the new leadership paradigm may suggest that senior managers become leading learners whose primary task is to support the design, implementation and follow-up of the learning of all others in the organisation. Where this has not been the case, as in two of the three examples given, the researchers have felt that the full potential of their research has not been achieved. Only at Kents Hill School, where the researcher was the most senior member of staff, have such barriers not arisen. Despite the belief of the practitioner researchers that they had achieved only partial success, the views of colleagues have been more optimistic and have concluded quite certainly that the work undertaken had results in both personal and organisational terms.

On the evidence presented here, one might conclude that two of the three institutions considered were not learning organisations. However, it may be that the concept of 'learning organisation' is an ideal type and, as with all such ideal types, no absolute example could be found. To become a learning organisation involves both attitudinal and process changes. The example of the tertiary college offers a demonstration of process which takes the organisation close to the ideal type. The formal procedure of circulating the results of research, considering them and translating them into an action plan ensures that no research can be ignored and not bear some fruit. However, where the results of the research imply cultural or attitudinal change, such a process may be inadequate to achieve what is required. It may be that on this dimension of change, the commitment and active involvement of the most senior staff is critical. The skill of the practitioner researcher may therefore lie in assessing the context in which the work is to take place and electing to focus his or her energies on a research area appropriate to the degree of support likely to be secured from the headteacher/principal. It is not that research cannot have a profound impact without the support and involvement of the headteacher, but rather if research is to have an impact in such a context, the selection of a research area which does not require such support is critical. The received orthodoxy is that a research focus should relate to organisational need. The evidence presented in this chapter suggests that this may be too limited an approach and further criteria may be needed for the selection of research aims, relating to micropolitical support.

3
_____

RE-APPRAISING ROLES
THROUGH RESEARCH

Marianne Coleman

INTRODUCTION – WHAT IS A ROLE?

The concept of role is generally taken to be more than a formal definition
of position or job description within a school or college:

> Roles are therefore defined in the relationships between positions in a
> structure expressed in the behaviours considered appropriate rather than
> merely in the designated positions themselves. (Ribbins, 1988, p. 58)

Role, and appropriate role behaviour, are very much defined by the
expectations of those who relate to the post-holder, these people are
known as the 'role set'. The number and variety of people in a role set will
vary, but will certainly include the subordinates and super-ordinates and
peers of the individual in the role. In the case of a teacher in a school, a
role set would also include students and their parents, for a college
lecturer the role set might expand to include local employers. Where the
members of the role set hold differing expectations, or the role itself has
internal ambiguities, the role holder may find that they are subject to role
stress. An individual role is a product of the relationship between the role
holder and their role set:

> Role definition is a constant process of negotiation, which involves not only
> the expectations of others, but how the individual perceives these expecta-
> tions, which he perceives as legitimate, and the manner in which he responds
> to them.
>
> (Maw, 1977, p. 95)

However important the perceptions of the role set, an individual will individualise his or her own role. Hall (1997) refers to the concepts of 'role-taking and role-making':

> the reasons why an individual behaves differently from his or her formal job description may derive from the individual's attempts to make the role his or her own, by fitting it to his or her own interpretation.
>
> (p. 63)

It therefore follows that the role of an individual will be affected by the view that person takes of their own role and also by the view that members of the role set take, both of the nature and content of the role and of the suitability of the individual for the role. These views in turn will be subject to past experience and to cultural and stereotypical expectations. For example, race, age or gender may impact on the way in which an individual operates within their role and will certainly affect how they are perceived by their role set. Whilst we may rationally accept that there is no reason why a woman should not be a leader, the stereotypical concept of the male as leader persists (Schein, 1994) and an unconscious expectation may be that women will hold supportive or pastoral roles.

Stereotypes affecting perception of the most suitable role for an individual may be particularly strong where both race and gender are concerned. Thompson (1992) reviewing equality issues in appraisal notes that: 'it is frequently assumed that black teachers will work only or largely with ethnic minority children' (p. 236). Interviews with black and ethnic female managers (Davidson, 1997) showed that:

> the majority of the sample when questioned about both gender and racial role stereotyping alignment at work, commonly complained of role imposition based primarily on the stereotypical image of females of their specific ethnic origin.
>
> (Davidson, 1997, p. 41)

For example, Afro-Caribbean and African women managers felt that they were expected to be an 'aggressive, black female mama', and Asian women that they were expected to be the stereotypical 'female timid Asian flower' (*ibid.*).

The nature of a role is that it is dynamic, and subject to changes. These changes may be due to a fresh role incumbent or to changes to expectations about the role whose origins might be either internal and external to an educational institution. For example, roles in a school or college are certain to be affected by major internal changes such as re-structuring or the appointment of a new headteacher or principal.

> In this process [of role definition] the head can be, and usually is, extremely powerful, because his [*sic*] expectations, whether formally laid down or not, affect the expectations that others are likely to have. Every head, therefore,

needs to consider how powerful he ought to be in the process of role definition, and how far others should be formally involved.

(Maw, 1977, p. 95)

There are many examples of how external changes may affect expectations about roles in education. An international trend towards increased school and college autonomy has impacted on the role of senior management and governors, increasing their range of responsibilities. The introduction of inspection, league tables and emphasis on increased school effectiveness in England and Wales has led to changes in the role of middle managers in schools, with greater stress on team management and monitoring rather than on the more mechanistic or administrative aspects of the role.

Hall (1997) refers to some of the wider external influences that lead to complications in the identification of the nature of management roles in particular:

> These difficulties arise from a number of sources, including the diversity of goals in education, teachers' perceptions of themselves as 'professionals' and the interaction of central government's prescriptions and individual teachers' interpretations. Additionally, there are the global changes that influence teachers' work and culture in the post-modern age.

(p. 62)

This chapter considers school- and college-based research that has investigated and re-appraised a number of roles. The data presented here were collected through interviews and questionnaires in the case study institutions. The first set of examples relate to the impact of internal and external changes in schools and colleges. In the first case study, the investigation of the role of the governors was inspired by a combination of internal problems and externally imposed changes in an English girls' secondary school. In the second, the investigation of the role of middle managers by a newly appointed principal in Northern Ireland was partly instigated by the new responsibilities that middle managers now face and partly used as a component of a strategy of the new head to gradually change the culture of his school. This section ends with a brief consideration of how a lecturer in a further education college used the appointment of a new middle manager to a new post in a college to consider the nature of this role and the expectations of the role set.

The final part of the chapter considers role in a different way, concentrating on the ways in which the factor of gender in particular may impact on the perceptions of both the role holder and the role set. Brief consideration is given to an evaluation of female middle managers in a college in Abu Dhabi and then to investigations of the different ways in which gender impacts on management roles in primary schools, special schools and in a Druze school in Israel.

THE IMPACT OF INSTITUTIONAL CHANGES AND EXTERNAL INFLUENCES ON ROLES

The Role of the Governors

In this school there was a range of influences, both internal and external, that led to a need for a re-examination of the role of the governors and their relationships with managers in the school. Internally, the most important change was the appointment of a new Headteacher. However, there was an unexpected financial crisis in this school, where:

> The governors had every cause to believe the school, which was high in the league tables and heavily oversubscribed, to be successful.

The crisis caused by a potentially large shortfall in the budget leading to redundancies, threw the responsibilities of the Governors into high relief. In this difficult set of circumstances, the Deputy Head, Kathy, decided to undertake a case study which focused on the role of the Governors and which would try to establish positive ways to move forward. For a variety of reasons, the Governors had not fully come to terms with their increased responsibilities resulting from statutory changes and the move to grant-maintained status:

> The previous Head believed that Governors should be kept at arm's length and told only the good news. This led to some complacency amongst the governing body. With a new Head and with the financial situation in dire straits it was a good opportunity to look at the role of the Governors. The new Head felt it was important for the Governors to begin to ask more questions and take up the reins. It came as a shock to some of them to know what was really going on.

The main method of investigation was interviews with the Governors, but Kathy was also aware that the governing body did little or no training and she used questionnaires to try to establish training needs. Looking to the future meant that she also found it useful to ask questions relating to the induction and general level of involvement of the new Governors. The formality of the Governors' meetings had tended to make them very long; the present Chair of Governors stated that:

> The meetings were formal and bureaucratic, also the Chairman was used to doing things his way, he knew so much more than us ... The Governors met twice a term for three hours and then there were sub-committee meetings as well but we weren't really talking about the pupils.

As a result of the investigation, Kathy made the following recommendations:

- the Governors to be provided with more literature about their role and responsibilities and a small library made available to them;
- improvements should be made to the agendas, standing orders and the circulation of papers for Governors' meetings;
- an induction pack should be developed for new Governors together with a new procedure for induction including the provision of a mentor;
- training priorities should be confirmed;
- the introduction of closer links with staff.

In addition, a summary of the research was given to the Governors. The view of the present Chair of Governors was that:

> What Kathy's work did was to force us to step back and see how we were handling the meetings. The fact is, it was her as an independent person and the formality of her doing the MBA which had impact and carried the weight. Everyone knew how much work Kathy had put in and she has no axe to grind.

More than a year on from the research on the role of Governors, most of the recommendations are in place. Many of them were quite practical in nature, such as the recommendations relating to the organisation of meetings, and the provision of induction packs, but the Chair of Governors considers that the recommendations have led to: 'getting a different attitude at Governor's meetings'. The view of a newly appointed teacher Governor was that:

> As a new teacher Governor I'm very impressed by how much work goes into it and how informed some of the Governors need to be. It has opened my eyes.

The revelation of the need for a re-examination of the Governors' role occurred as a result of a financial crisis and at a time when a new head was appointed. There was therefore a real impetus for changes to occur. Kathy recognised that:

> Some things would have happened anyway but my research was a bit of a catalyst.

Kathy went on to further research involving Governors and their relationship with middle managers, aiming to improve the information links between the two and to enhance the role that both play in the process of development planning.

The Role of Middle Managers

Daniel was appointed as the Principal of the College in 1995, and as part of his decision to change the culture of the school towards a more collaborative and learner-centred approach, undertook a study of middle managers in the school: 'We wanted to devolve power to middle managers and support them here.' He was also aware that a rather narrow view of the role of academic middle managers was taken in the school.

The influence of middle managers, particularly heads of department, has long been recognised:

> The vital importance of the role of the head of department is that it lies at the heart of the educational process ... whether a student achieves or under-achieves is largely dependent on the quality of planning, execution and evaluation that takes place within individual departments... yet, in the majority of schools the full potential of the role has not been developed.
>
> (HMI Wales, 1985)

The role of middle managers has a number of facets. Bennett (1995) identifies elements of the role as including: responsibility for curriculum; responsibility for the work of others; responsibility for contributing to whole-school activities and responsibility for finance and resources. In recent research on academic middle managers, Wise (1997) identifies a four-fold classification of tasks: administrative; managerial; academic and educational.

At the time of the investigation, the expectation of middle managers in St Malachy's College was that:

> the essential role of the head of department was limited to administrative tasks – such as managing resources, allocating classes and choosing syllabuses for public exams.

In this, St Malachy's was little different to the schools researched by Bennett (1995) who concluded that for most middle managers:

> There was a clear culture in the language of the job descriptions that the post holders would be in charge of delivering what was laid down rather than involved in developing what was to be done, overseeing and ordering what their teams did rather than developing the work in a constructive or collaborative way. There was little reference to leadership and development, almost none to motivating and encouraging staff, and much to organising and implementing.
>
> (Bennett, 1995, p. 116)

As part of the move towards a change in culture, Daniel wanted to emphasise the more educational and academic parts of the role of the middle managers, and in particular to encourage there being a 'clearer focus on the management of teaching and learning'.

The method of investigation adopted was a questionnaire to all 23 heads of department. The response rate was good, Daniel commenting that 'staff tend to respond to the Principal!' The key findings were that:

- where it had been introduced, collaborative team working was seen to be effective;
- senior management should increase levels of communication and

consultation;

- the clarification of roles was essential, but that the development of this clarification should be collaborative;
- there was a need for training in key skills such as handling meetings and using statistics (this need was linked to the decision to be involved with Investors in People);
- middle managers need appropriate time to manage, the implication may be that some senior managers will have less non-teaching time;
- a collaboratively produced development plan will provide an appropriate context for middle managers to manage.

In all this it was recognised that change takes time and that 'there is much institutional lethargy to overcome'.

Reviewing the results of the investigation, a year after it was carried out, the verdict was generally good. Daniel felt that the general support for staff implied in many of the findings 'has been taken on board' and that 'there is a clear understanding of the job description for Heads of Year'. However, for a single investigation that was part of an overall effort to change the culture of the school it was:

> hard to say which specific recommendations came from this assignment because all the assignments, the reading and the Investors in People input are all working in the same way.

A particular benefit to Daniel of the investigations he carries out in the school is in furthering his own collaborative relationship with staff: 'It's telling them "you can trust me, I will listen to what you're saying".' In addition, planning can be based on data collected in the school, rather than what Daniel calls 'wishful thinking'.

One problem that the research has not affected is finding the appropriate time to give to middle managers to manage. The external pressure on the school budget for the provision of IT makes it difficult to cut down on teaching periods and allow staff more time to manage. James, a senior manager in the school, who has worked under previous heads, recognised the benefits of the changes brought about through the work of the new Principal but was also aware of the rather intractable nature of the problem of providing middle managers with sufficient time to manage:

> Over the last few years, many teachers in the school have developed a more positive attitude to management and are working more effectively in teams. As a member of Daniel's Senior Management Team I share his vision of management but have to acknowledge that there is a genuine problem for teachers in the current climate of rapid educational change. Many teachers, in all schools, have experienced an increased workload and are frustrated (and often stressed) because they do not have enough time to carry out effectively all the tasks they are expected to do.

The difficulties in changing the culture of middle management are not underestimated, and James identified the sometimes variable nature of the reaction of middle managers to the changes:

> Some teachers are keen to become involved in decision-making by participating in middle management committees etc. but others find this responsibility onerous. Some teachers do not want to become involved in whole-school development issues – they see their role as that of classroom teacher.

The practical effects of the research carried out in a school by a key change agent, in this case the Principal, are obvious:

> We've gone for a process leading to the Investors in People award. The information gathered from all the work has helped to inform our own process. We are further down the line, because of the research, than other schools involved in the exercise. It informs our whole perspective of what we are as a school, helping us to maintain our special qualities. It also provides us with a clear analysis of staff development needs and this extends beyond the teaching staff to all staff involved in the school community.

However, the effects must be seen as part of a larger move on the part of a head described as 'charismatic' by one of his senior managers, towards introducing a collaborative and learning culture within the school.

Middle Management Research in a Further Education College

The effect of a similar investigation into the roles of middle management in a College of Further Education in England was less impressive. This may owe something to the fact that the researcher did not hold a senior role in the college, and that his efforts appear as an individual exercise, rather than integrated into a larger co-ordinated plan as in the case of St Malachy's.

In this case the research was intended to develop a clearer understanding of how a change in expectations of a new middle management role, that of School Manager (a School here means a sub-section of a faculty), and the appointment of a new person to this role, would impact on the different members of the role set, that is specifically the senior managers and the staff of the School to be headed by the new appointee.

The main findings of this research indicated that 'mixed messages' were apparent in relation to the new role, for example:

> The staff rated highly the ability to be able to make decisions and to deal with routine day-to-day maintenance functions, and yet there is little if anything in the job descriptions which allocates exposure to this area of the job.

There is less urgency than the staff would like in relation to the 'entrepreneur' role.

It is clear that neither the School Manager nor the Head of Faculty are in jobs that they want and both are wishing that it was different.

The lecturer who undertook this investigation reported back that:

the completed assignment received no response, neither from my Head of Faculty, the Head of School (the subject of the enquiry), nor any member of the College's senior management team.

In this case the benefit from the investigation could only be expressed in terms of personal achievement and the research did not appear to impact in any way on the institution.

THE IMPACT OF GENDER ON THE PERCEPTIONS OF BOTH THE ROLE HOLDER AND THE ROLE SET

The Management Style of Female Middle Managers in a College

An investigation of middle managers in one of the Higher Colleges of Technology in Abu Dhabi focused only on female managers, with the major concern being that of management style. This study was undertaken within the context of the under-representation of women in management in the College which raises the question that there may be preconceptions about the roles that are suitable for women. Although no recommendations were formally made as a result of this investigation, which took the form of semi-structured interviews and questionnaires, the study concluded that:

their (women managers') style was consultative and participatory and further work should be carried out to find out *why* women are under-represented at management level.

No specific management action was taken in the College as a result of this research. However, it was known that other students following the same distance learning course for the MBA in Educational Management had carried out further and related research in the same subject area. Obviously, research can only play a small part in any change in the complex relationship of factors that underlie the perceptions of the suitability of women for management roles. In addition, the researcher had not intended that her research would lead to any recommendations, commenting that the benefit to her was 'Personal enjoyment at completing an interesting piece of research.'

However, although no benefits were recognised by the institution, the female middle managers who were interviewed in the research were advantaged by the research which brought them a fresh understanding of their own roles:

> The process of finding out about their staff's opinion of them was very heartening to the supervisors interviewed (under scrutiny). In a way, it was the first time they had had full performance evaluation feedback on themselves.

The Implications of Gender for the Role of Primary Headteacher

Many small scale research projects are undertaken in an attempt to directly improve an aspect of the school or college. Their relative success or failure will depend on a variety of factors explored elsewhere in this book. However, some research is undertaken in a more reflective mood, to explore concepts and in so doing enlighten the researcher and probably those who take part in the research. In the long run this type of research may have an impact on the school or college where it has been undertaken, or it may affect the management or leadership style of the individual, thereby impacting indirectly on their present and future places of work.

In this investigation, Martin, a primary school headteacher, decided to explore concepts of leadership and their relationship to gender. There were two underlying motivations for doing this. One was knowing that many of those factors that are now identified with effective management may also be those that can be termed 'feminine' and that these qualities are likely to be found more often in women than in men:

> The game is changing, the way people motivate, lead and manage is changing as well. Management is seen as masculine but we could move towards the situation where leadership and management may be seen as feminine.

The other factor motivating this enquiry was the gender inequity of management in primary education. Martin conducted this study in the context of primary education in England and Wales, where over 80 per cent of teachers are women and 50 per cent of headteachers are men (DfEE, 1997).

> The fact is that the number of men who are primary teachers is small and the number of men heads is shockingly large. As a male head working with a primarily female group of colleagues I felt it was important that I understand the motives and motivation of the women I'm working with. In September I start my third headship, it's a large school, 700 children and over 70 staff, teachers and support staff and there are no men there except for me.

In order to explore some of the ways in which gender affects the role of the primary school headteacher, Martin undertook interviews with six primary heads from the same West London local education authority. Three were men and three were women. Martin based his interview on similar interviews carried out with female secondary headteachers (Coleman, 1996) but his investigation focused on the identification and explanation of traits drawn from the feminine and masculine paradigms developed by Gray (1993), also used by Coleman (1996).

The main finding of this small scale piece of research was that the male headteachers were more likely to identify themselves as having 'feminine' traits, the identification of 'masculine' traits being more common amongst the women. Martin offers two possible hypotheses for the predominance of 'feminine' traits amongst the men:

> This could be due to a sort of 'feminisation' process caused by spending many years working in a female culture or it could be that male headteachers *always* had a strong 'feminine' side, and that the 'nurturing' aspects deep in their nature was a key factor in their decision to become teachers of young children.

One of the interviewed heads, Barbara, referred to the need for both men and women to take on traits that relate to their role and the expectations of the role set:

> Male colleague heads feel that they have had to learn the traits that would normally be attributed to females. As a female headteacher I think I have had to take on male traits. Things like being more objective and not taking things personally, being more analytical.

Within this research it was the women who tended to identify a greater range of traits from both the masculine and feminine categories, and could therefore be labelled as 'androgynous' leaders, those identified as:

> able to respond more effectively than either masculine or feminine individuals to a wide variety of situations.

(Ferrario, 1994, p. 116)

However, the belief that a feminine management style was appropriate to modern management in a primary school was endorsed by Alan, one of the male heads:

> It seems that I came out strongly on feminine characteristics and it was interesting that that was the case. I wonder if it is because I work in a predominantly female environment? It made me affirm the values that I am holding. I identified the values with the ones that were needed in leadership in the 21st century.

The importance of having male role models was commented upon by Barbara whose staff of 18 includes the high proportion of five male teachers. She speculated that the fact that the girls are not out-performing the boys at her school might be influenced by having male role models and felt that the balance in the staff makes the atmosphere 'more positive' for both children and staff.

Gender thus emerges as an important factor relating to the role of leader, and indeed to the role of the teacher, in the primary school. Possibly the main finding emerging from this piece of small scale qualitative research is that awareness of gender traits and issues does impact in a variety of ways on these headteachers. In this case the headteachers showed a sophisticated awareness of current management thinking and of the ways in which gender related factors might impinge on their own understanding of their roles.

Martin did not set out to make recommendations, but only to explore concepts for his own development; this exploration was also useful to the interviewed heads who commented on the benefits that they obtained from reflecting on their leadership style. However, Martin did make one suggestion in the light of his findings, and that was for further reflection and research. He felt that there was a:

> need to look at the denial of self for men in certain environments. There is more of an argument for cultural transformation, to make sure that everybody feels they can express both masculine and feminine aspects of their character.

The gender dimensions of the role of primary school head were revealed as more complex than might have been thought and worthy of further research.

The Impact of Gender on the Role Perception of Women Special School Headteachers

As the Headteacher of a special school, Joyce was aware that although men came into headship of special schools, they did not stay. Most of her colleagues and her staff were female. Her investigation was carried out through an analysis of the statistics relating to headship in Warwickshire Special Schools from 1979 to 1996, and through in-depth interviews with five female special school heads based on a review of relevant literature. The purpose of the research could be related to the lack of confidence that is often identified with women (Shakeshaft, 1989; Al Khalifa, 1992). The research was carried out in order to clarify and validate her own role as a female head with female colleagues:

> it was about confidence, and reassurance that the female bit is OK ... I and the other heads I interviewed suffer from a lack of confidence and need reassurance that we're doing a good job.

One of the heads interviewed, Sheila commented that the feedback from the research:

showed us more about the different ways in which we manage, and allows us to share in relation to the strategies we use in the management role.

Allied to the need for clarification and reassurance as female leaders there was a concern about human resource management:

> There were management needs, personnel issues, role models. It reaffirmed for me that what was important was that it was the best person for the job and gender was irrelevant. It would have been nice to have had a high flying male, but it didn't happen at that time.

Benefits accruing from the research therefore related both to the reinforcement of confidence on the part of herself and her colleagues to whom she fed back the results, but also to aspects of professional development. In this, Joyce saw her own work on the MBA as acting as an example to others, giving her weight in her desire to promote the idea of lifelong learning to her staff.

Her research led her to a realisation of the importance of mentoring, particularly in the career development of women; a finding that reinforces the need to build confidence and may provide appropriate professional development both to mentor and protégé:

> Mentoring is the key. Loads of women lack the confidence that they need to plan ahead.

This thinking was endorsed by Sheila, who, as a result of the feedback from Joyce on the importance of mentoring, commented:

> I see it as one of my roles with my colleagues, to be there for them. I just wish there was something in place for me.

As in the research in West London primary schools, the focus for this piece of research was related to understanding the impact of gender on management and leadership roles, but again it was against a background where men and women are disproportionately represented, highlighting the relevance of gender to role.

Research on gender inequality in educational management is often carried out, as in the examples above, to clarify their own understanding of the impact of gender on role or on styles of management. However, on a national and international basis, culturally imbued stereotypes and subtle forms of discrimination may influence the career progress of women (Coleman, 1994). In the final example in this chapter, the culture in question rules out the possibility of women holding management positions at present.

Role Stress Experienced by Women Teachers
in a Druze School in Israel

Salman Falah, working in a Druze school in Israel, undertook a series of telephone interviews with a sample of 25 Druze and Arab women teachers, since there are no women managers in his school. The purpose of the research was to investigate the views of the women and to relate them to stress within their roles. Role stress may result from conflicting expectations from members of the role set. In this society, the treatment of women was termed: 'very conservative and based on religious traditions'. It is therefore likely that professional women would be subject to role stress in attempting to fully carry out expectations of others in both their home and professional life. In commenting on the personal benefit he experienced in undertaking this research Salman stated that:

> I received a deeper understanding of how women view their position as professionals and as women in the Druze community. I became more aware of the conflict between job demands and family demands.

Following his findings being presented to the senior managers in the school, a decision has been made that: 'now women are allowed to accompany girl students on field trips.' A small step for the female teachers and students, but one that can be directly traced to the research. In addition, there may have been some personal benefit for the women who were interviewed in outlining the nature of their role stress:

> I believe that the women teachers who participated in the study benefited in being able to express themselves more openly concerning the conflicts in their professional and personal lives.

The effects of research relating to role, or any other area, will vary according to the purpose and extent of the research and the cultural factors that may be internal to the school or college. In addition, the wider cultural context will have an impact on both the focus and the process of research projects.

REAPPRAISING ROLES

Small scale research investigations may be particularly appropriate for the investigation and reappraisal of roles as they change and develop. The nature of a role is that it is somewhat context bound. Generalisations from large scale research may provide the background in which to set a specific role, but the development of a particular role such as that of a middle manager will be influenced by the range of circumstances in which the individual is operating. In the case of St Malachy's College, the role of the middle manager was being developed within a changing culture of collaboration, the process of research itself contributing to the changing culture. In the girls' grammar school, the pressure to reappraise the role of the governors arose from the statutory changes in the powers and responsibilities of the governors, but the proximate causes were the internal changes caused by the financial crisis and the appointment of a new head. Research enabled the development of practical measures to improve both the understanding of Governors and the processes of governance. However, small-scale research that takes place without a measure of support from senior management seems unlikely to have any impact except on the researcher unless the area researched falls within the range of their own influence.

Whatever the role, the perceptions of those in a role set will be affected by factors such as the gender of the role holder. Research that takes gender into account will aim to dispel some of the stereotypes relating to gender that may accrue to an individual or to the role that they play. The research on gender and its effects on leadership roles undertaken in the primary and special schools in England sought to reappraise the effect of gender on leadership and clarify some of the related issues. The research on the role stress of women in a Druze school appears to have had a limited but real impact in both practical terms and in raising awareness of both the researcher and those interviewed.

4

INFLUENCING THE MANAGEMENT OF THE CURRICULUM

Jacky Lumby

INTRODUCTION

Many writers have posited a dislocation between an education system which is in evolution and technology which is in revolution (Edwards, 1997; Hargeaves, 1997; Davies, 1997). Compounding the impact of the technological revolution, the implications of changing demography and working practices have resulted in a shift in emphasis to education as a lifelong activity which is likely to occur in a more dispersed way than previously, breaking the bounds of schools and colleges, and happening in the home and workplace as an ongoing feature. These shifts amount to change on a scale which has outstripped the capacity of educators, governments and available resources to keep pace. The difficulties faced by schools and colleges in finding the funds to equip themselves with technology and to use it effectively for teaching and learning is a commonly rehearsed theme. Less high profile is the perhaps more fundamental struggle to address what such changes mean in human terms. Supportive and guiding relationships with educators are still axiomatic, but the nature of the relationship may be undergoing metamorphosis. The ultimate aim of equipping each student to take a constructive and enjoyable role in society and to fulfil individual potential remains unchallenged. The means of achieving this end is under scrutiny. Questions include: what are the best means of enabling independent learning? Is the traditional divide between pastoral and academic roles still valid? If much learning will take place outside the educational organisation, using information technology in the home and beyond in cyber cafes, how can a holistic and coherent experience of learning be achieved? How can funds be managed to achieve a learning-based curriculum?

This chapter focuses on four examples of lecturers using research to develop the curriculum. The focus of the chapter is exclusively on further education, because it is within this sector that changes in response to the context described have been most pronounced. The four colleges, two further education colleges and one sixth form college in England and one technical college in the United Arab Emirates are a convenience sample chosen to explore the theme of research used to meet the challenge of the new demands on the curriculum. Rugby College had established a Learning Resources Centre and wished to make it central to learning. Mereside Sixth Form College explored how student progress could be monitored through a value added system in a way that supported teaching and learning, rather than the contrary. A technical college in the United Arab Emirates examined the structures which allowed assessment of the appropriate curriculum in relation to the needs of employers. Loughborough College participated in a national research project to focus on re-examining the role of tutors in supporting and managing learning. Each of these illustrates one aspect of possible adjustments to ensure that the curriculum meets the needs of the individual student and the economy, and establishes teaching and learning in a mode credible for the 21st century.

DEVELOPING A LEARNING RESOURCE CENTRE

The focus of the research in Rugby College was the Learning Resource Centre, which was subject to differing views on its purpose and use. The College appointed a new manager of the Centre to carry forward development. The manager had reached the final stage of her MBA with Leicester University and aimed to use the dissertation to construct a model of student use of the facility, identifying key issues influencing access and use. No accepted pattern of management of such facilities existed within the sector, and a model which could identify the factors encouraging productive use was potentially of great value. The dissertation concluded by recommending a management model for the Centre. The manager herself, the Head of the Faculty with responsibility for the Centre and the Curriculum Manager for Business Studies, who was also a course team leader and a member of the college Survey Group, were interviewed to gather their differing perspectives on the research and its impact.

At the time of the manager's appointment the Learning Resource Centre was relatively new and staff and students were uncertain of its use and value:

> Some staff saw it as cost cutting in terms of reducing contact time but what we were doing was forcing people to look at different ways in which to deliver the curriculum and to use the Learning Resource Centre as a vehicle for that. We were also aware of students, as contact hours have been reduced over the years, drifting off home, going into town, sitting around the College and not using their free time, so we decided we wanted to give them timetabled private study in the Learning Resource Centre so that they would use their private study more constructively.
>
> (Head of Faculty)

> We'd had experience in the past where the term 'private study' was an automatic flag to students which meant they didn't have to be there. When we were initially discussing the development of the Learning Resources area there were concerns that we would spend a lot of time and resources developing something that students wouldn't use. The second concern was around the area of who would co-ordinate the whole thing, what would its role be, how would its link to students and their learning be made? It was at that time just a library ... at the start our fears appeared to be founded because there were large numbers of students who said they were in the Resources area but when we looked at the registers in fact they weren't there. Partly I suppose because students didn't really understand what it was all about even though we had sat them down and explained the whole thing to them.
>
> (Curriculum Manager)

The Learning Resource Centre was consequently subject to hopes and fears of how it might develop. The newly appointed Learning Resources Manager also brought a personal context. Having moved from a previous role as Head of School in another college, with a consequent drop in salary and status, the Manager felt the need to do a 'PR job' convincing people of her capacity not only to contribute, but to lead. Academically she felt rusty, having not done certificated study for over 20 years, and the MBA, and particularly the sustained work of the dissertation, was an opportunity to apply her intellect. There was also a need for a vehicle to enforce reflection:

> When you're on your feet and busy in a facility like this, you think in odd snatches and then wake up at two in the morning and think of a further few snatches. I wanted to force myself to approach things logically, to take time to do some investigation ... it was new for all of us when we were building up the Learning Resource Centres around the country. There was a desperate need for time to sit and think, how does it fit with this organisation, because there was no accepted model, there was no rule book.
>
> (Learning Resources Manager)

The Head of Faculty, pleased with appointing a person of such ability, recognised the need to ensure that challenges were set to provide motivation and retention and also believed that the college could only benefit from the research in understanding better how the Learning Resource Centre might develop.

The reasons for undertaking the research were therefore a mix of personal and organisational. The senior management was already committed to the idea of enriching and developing students' use of study time, but were uncertain of how to go forward. The Learning Resources Manager was motivated by both personal and organisational development needs. Other staff, through representation on the Survey Group, also wished to verify assumptions about the use of the Centre and identify possible development.

The research method chosen was a survey by questionnaire to allow modelling. This latter is not used very frequently by practitioners. The survey of Leicester MBA students identified that questionnaires, used by 78 per cent of respondents, and interviews, used by 49 per cent, were by far the most common research tools employed. This dissertation was the only example of the use of modelling. Cohen and Manion (1994, p. 16) describe models as an 'explanatory scheme ... often characterized by the use of analogies to give a more graphic or visual representation of a particular phenomenon'. In other words, the elements involved in a real phenomenon, the relationship between the elements, and the possible outcomes are represented visually in such a way as to clarify what is happening and sometimes how changing any of the elements may change the outcomes. In this way a model may make a process clearer and provide a basis for decision as to how to manage the elements involved. Modelling was chosen by this researcher because of its capacity to encompass many factors and offer the possibility of discerning a pattern, thereby identifying clear routes for development.

During the implementation of the research, the Learning Resources Manager enjoyed a supportive relationship with the Head of Faculty. The latter discussed the use of the dissertation to develop the Centre and thereafter, rather than being closely involved, provided a positive environment:

> It was casual, just constant approval, not with the nuts and bolts of what questions I was asking in the survey or even going through the dissertation in detail when I'd written it but the steady knowledge that she knew that this was underlying the progress that the College wanted to make, though bottom line – it was vastly in the interests of the College that I should do research.
>
> (Learning Resources Manager)

Students too provided motivation:

> I had ... I think, admiration from the people who gathered what I was doing. That actually included the students, both mature students and the younger ones who thought, my gosh, here's a nearly grey-haired lady writing dissertations! It gave them a bit of hope.
>
> (Learning Resources Manager)

The outcomes of the research were both personal and organisational. For the Learning Resources Manager, the process provided a new lease of energy and interest, and enhanced her status and relationships with students and staff:

> It just gave me a lift when I needed it. I'm coming up to 50. I was looking for a career change, going with the research, going alongside the research, getting myself established here, gaining the respect of a new cohort of staff, gave me the 'Philosan' boost if you like.
>
> (Learning Resources Manager)

There were also outcomes for the organisation. The dissertation concluded by producing a model for the management of the Learning Resource Centre and a checklist of strategies for its adoption. The efforts to implement the strategies have brought results. There were conceptual and attitudinal changes, though it was clear that not all staff had yet been convinced of the value and appropriateness of the investment in the Learning Resource Centre. There was some movement towards staff feeling that the Centre was integral to their work, and not an inessential bolt-on. At an instrumental level, the dissertation was used as the justification for considerable investment and expansion of the Centre, leading to use by more students, including those such as engineering and music students, whose previous use had been minimal. Staff involved in the former library and Learning Resource Centre staff are moving towards some multi-skilling, and broadening their role. The impact has therefore been felt as physical expansion, more staff and students using the Centre in a proactive way and the role of Centre staff developing.

> Two years ago it was purely and simply a library. It's now become a one stop centre to support student learning with access to computers and technology. In the past students went to the library and they had to get together their own material and be responsible for their own work. They were responsible for their own mistakes. It's now moved from a centre for study to a centre for student support where there's a lot more proactive involvement in students' learning.
>
> (Curriculum Manager)

The conditions which enabled the research to bear fruit were multiple. Both the Learning Resources Manager and the Head of Faculty were clear that the research was not the sole cause of the development. Many of the things might have happened without the research, but:

it would have been far more haphazard. I would have been less confident. In going back to the situation of a new college, new colleagues and the feeling that you've got to get it right or you'll blow it, the research was vital.

(Learning Resources Manager)

The Head of Faculty used the dissertation to drive forward development:

> It was interesting and informative. It confirmed many of the things we'd been talking about. It was also a useful management tool for discussion with the rest of the Executive, particularly the Principal, in terms of expanding the Learning Resource Centre. The timing was quite good ... I copied sections of it as part of a paper to the Executive to suggest we need to expand this area. This is what it can do for us. These are the benefits. We need to invest in this and we did.

(Head of Faculty)

The Curriculum Manager saw the value of the research as ensuring that the college avoided the danger of making assumptions about student needs and wants. The Learning Resources Manager and the Head of Faculty both saw the active and persistent pursuit of the outcomes of the research as key:

> Nobody, but nobody is going to sit down and read this research from cover to cover. You might say that's a big disappointment in my life but it's not, though colleagues have dipped in and seen odd bits, though very few. It's me disseminating what I've learnt, teaching people what I've learnt, otherwise they would lose a lot.

(Learning Resources Manager)

Her belief was that the college had 'got a lot of thinking done for free' and quick results. The evidence of the research, translated through the advocacy of the Head of Faculty, was the foundation of further investment:

> There was evidence in the research which backed up what she was asking for. She wasn't saying I want this because I fancy it, but I want it because I can prove it.

(Head of Faculty)

The partnership between the Head of Faculty and the Learning Resources Manager resulted in a developmental base, with the Learning Resources Manager disseminating and 'teaching' staff, and a micropolitical base, where the Head of Faculty saw her advocacy as perhaps making a difference. Asked what factors ensured the research was used fully, she responded:

> The fact that she [the Learning Resources Manager] made sure that I had a copy of it. The fact that I valued her opinion, her skills and her ability and took the time to actually read it. I felt that when we recruited her it was quite a coup to have found somebody who was so able. She had practical skills and intellectual skills and I valued what she did. It was our relationship. Had she sent it to the Principal he may well have chosen to take note of it and act on it. I'd like to think that my involvement made some difference.

(Head of Faculty)

Both members of the partnership valued each other, and contributed towards a common goal. The Learning Resources Manager chose to focus her work on achieving the vision set by senior management. The Head of Faculty adopted a management style which supported and disseminated. In this she acted as a patron of the research:

> It's been a partnership. There are a lot of things I couldn't have done without her and she certainly made a difference in that she shared the vision that we had and she has actually put it into place. I suppose what I have had to do is persuade the Executive, encourage the Executive once they had the vision, to put its money where its mouth is. Having a representative on the Senior Executive has been helpful.
>
> (Head of Faculty)

The quality of the research was the basis for action, but it is clear that other factors produced the conceptual and instrumental outcomes. The two factors identified by Fullan (1994) as critical to curriculum change, pressure and support, were enacted through the partnership. The whole process was centred on a common vision, also suggested as axiomatic to strategic development (Senge, 1990). This example of practitioner research suggests that it is the context in which research is undertaken, rather than the nature of the research itself, which will ensure that there is an impact at an organisational level.

USING A VALUE ADDED SYSTEM

The researcher at Mereside Sixth Form College was a Business Studies teacher, who has since left the college as one of a number of redundancies which happened in the period immediately following the conclusion of the research. Because he is no longer employed there, it was not possible to interview others, so the views expressed reflect just one perspective. The college is referred to by a pseudonym. The research raises some interesting issues and so has been included, despite the limitations described.

The starting point for the teacher was his anxiety that the use of the value added Advanced Level Information System (ALIS) and its link to newly introduced quality systems might be working to the detriment of students and staff. The ALIS system was being used to predict future grades on the basis of GCSE results without any consideration of other factors which might affect a student's performance:

> This approach had been developed very much on a basic level. It was very much a case of 'Well this is what you should have got and you didn't'. Teachers were being pressured into trying to achieve results which some students simply weren't able to achieve.

He feared that the situation was arising where Heads of Department might attempt to move students elsewhere when they looked unlikely to achieve their predicted grades, thereby avoiding the appearance of underachievement. The research was intended to explore if the system could be used sensitively to support rather than exert negative pressure. It was also hoped that in a personal sense the research might help the teacher identify:

> areas in which I should concentrate which would be a more effective use of my time, in developing students to get the best grade they're capable of.

An action research approach was selected with the fundamental aim of improving practice. A survey was conducted involving the Principal, the Director of Studies, two Heads of Department and 20 'A' level Business Studies students.

The actual process of the research started positively with interest and support from senior management, but was overtaken by other events:

> I think that initially they were interested in what I was trying to do, they being the Principal and the Director of Studies. The Director of Studies I think took a little more interest, in that he used to be the Head of Business Studies, and so I knew him quite well and also it fell upon him to introduce all these things like quality assurance and so on, so he was quite interested to see what I came up with. Support in other ways ... well, I was very much left to get on with it myself and in the end they didn't pay very much attention. I did give them a copy but I don't know if anybody read it because various other circumstances arose in the College to do with finance and there were a lot of redundancies that came up at that point, so that was the main issue at the time.

Despite the focus of the college being diverted to deal with redundancies, the research appears to have produced a number of outcomes. On a personal level, the researcher found the process helped him improve his classroom practice, by aiding him in refining his personal use of the ALIS system, moving beyond comparing predicted grades and performance to a more sophisticated understanding of the range of factors which might support or impede students in fulfilling their potential. This personal development was built on the understanding gained from interviewing a number of people in the college:

> I think that actually doing the assignment, the action research part of it ... got me out there and I learned a lot of things, interviewing people and trying to look at a lot of interviews first hand. The results did help me very much to concentrate on what I was doing in the classroom.

The research was also a factor in organisational change. One of the recommendations of the research was that joint task groups should be established to bridge the pastoral and academic roles:

Just before I left they decided to implement that, for a number of other reasons as well, and they actually re-structured the whole College. They now have joint Curriculum Heads and Pastoral Heads so that they now have a multi-functional role and can try and combine the two areas which were in conflict in certain circumstances.

There was also some awareness-raising amongst staff. The recommendation that more information about ALIS be circulated was implemented, but met with little enthusiasm, staff viewing the papers with suspicion as involving them in yet more work. The discussions with the researcher during the research process did engender interest, but was again overtaken by staff preoccupation with their security:

> Personally I think the research I did was of enormous benefit in that I think, by going about and questioning people, it made them think about how they approach their students. I was very much on a crusade about how do we get students from one point to another ... as effectively as possible, but again it tended to fade out when they thought, my job's on the line.

In line with the experience of Rugby College, it is clear that the recommendations which were implemented did not happen solely because of the research. As the researcher confirmed, the task groups were established for 'a number of other reasons as well'. His impression was that the context resulted in a shift of focus from the curriculum to finance and that the research was open to be used to provide an acceptable face for changes which were really driven by unpalatable financial realities. Research is vulnerable to political manipulation, in that, as in this case, recommendations which suggest restructuring and some elision of roles in order to achieve improvements in teaching and learning, can also be used to justify restructuring which relates to financial considerations. This is not to suggest that senior staff acted cynically, but rather to point out that the interpretation of the decision to act on the recommendations resulting from research may be subject to various interpretations. This ambivalence was felt by the researcher himself:

> I was a bit up and down about the whole thing at the end of it. I thought I'd got somewhere with the piece of research but because of circumstances it didn't go as far as I would have liked and the bits that did go and were implemented perhaps weren't implemented for what I considered the right reasons, probably out of necessity because of the financial constraints.

The question which arises is whether the motivation for the implementation of the recommendations, such as establishing the task groups, matters. Further follow up investigation would be needed to explore whether the micropolitical context of the college, and members' perception of the justification for the groups, undermined their efficacy or not. Certainly, even in very difficult circumstances, where staff were understandably preoccupied and anxious, the research still bore some fruit, if less than might otherwise have been the case.

THE CURRICULUM DEVELOPMENT PROCESS

The researcher in this case example was a teacher of electronics in the Faculty of Electronics in a college in the United Arab Emirates, studying for the MBA in Educational Management with Leicester University. He had felt the need to explore a number of curriculum changes which had been made, to understand why they had happened, if the results led to an appropriate curriculum and how the teaching staff could contribute to the curriculum development process. As will emerge, the particular culture of the college, allied to distance, meant that it was not possible to speak to others in the organisation, but minutes of Course Co-ordinators' meetings were used to triangulate the perceptions of the researcher on the outcomes of the research. The focus in this example is another key area of curriculum development, understanding the expectations and needs of those external to the organisation, and the relationship of these to the process of internal curriculum development.

The start point of this piece of research was the need to feel confidence in the curriculum:

> There had been a number of curriculum changes and I was interested to learn why the changes had been made. This was relevant to my area of teaching. I needed to understand the validity of the changes that were being made as it was important to me to feel I was teaching the appropriate curriculum to students. I felt that to receive international accreditation and credibility we needed to have an appropriate curriculum.

A case study approach was chosen, as the investigation concerned a real happening in the institution, and there were multiple sources of documentary evidence and individual perceptions that could be used to build up a rich picture. The context in which the research took place was one where the actual process of studying for a degree was not viewed as necessarily eliciting support. People would be supportive if they perceived the work was endorsed by managers, but not if it was seen to be part of a process of individual study:

> It was endorsed by senior management. It was better for me not to admit that the work I was doing was actually for my degree. The Director and the Engineering Manager were both very supportive but it was difficult to ask them for support as one cannot be seen to be going to one's superiors to ask for support too often. The administration and most people (colleagues, support staff and students) are very helpful and supportive. Some people will not

respond to questionnaires if they know that they are for a degree. There must
be an incentive for them to respond such as a request from administration.

The context was therefore a bureaucratic culture, where curriculum
change might be introduced without the involvement of teaching staff, and
where activity needed to be underpinned by a formal recognition of its
acceptability. There was also an assumption that work undertaken for
personal accreditation, such as a degree, was unlikely to bring any
benefits for the organisation:

> If I tell them [college staff] that I am doing this research as an assignment for
> an MBA, they will not care much. If I tell them that I am doing a research for
> the benefit of our college, they will care more about questionnaires, interviews
> and resources.

In this environment, the need for the researcher to establish the intended
organisational benefits with all those who might be involved was
consequently critical.

The case study led to a conclusion that the current system of curriculum
development was focused on teaching rather than learning. Course
outlines were rewritten using Bloom's (1956) taxonomy, a typology of
different intellectual skill levels, and then sent to the course team, which
usually provided no feedback but just implemented the changes. The
views of industry, but not those of teaching staff or students, were taken
into account. The role of the Engineering Curriculum Manager was largely
administrative. The researcher concluded that 'in order to shift from the
teaching paradigm to the learning paradigm' changes needed to take
place, including the establishment of a systematic process of course review
and development by specialised committees, including the input of those
who would teach the programme and programme supervisors. The views
of employers should be taken into account but should not be the only
opinions used. There were also recommendations concerning the actual
content of the curriculum and the resources needed, as no suitable
textbook was then current.

The assignment was read by 'the concerned people' and the researcher
reported findings and recommendations at meetings. This internal
dissemination process began to bring about change. The support of the
Engineering Manager was particularly helpful in forwarding the change.
Minutes of the Course Co-ordinators' meeting show that the course has been
restructured to reflect appropriate content and practical elements, a simple
course textbook has been produced, and the specialised committees have
begun the process of evaluation. Financial considerations have meant that
not all that was recommended has been possible. Nevertheless, the culture
of the management of the curriculum has shifted considerably from one
where senior committees could write and hand down courses for delivery, to

one where those closest to the teaching and learning are more involved. Personally the researcher has gained in feeling more confident and committed to the curriculum content he must teach. Even in a context where a bureaucratic culture was well established, and support for the researcher's individual study could not be assumed, the research has proved a lever for conceptual and instrumental change resulting in a curriculum paradigm shift within the programme area of electronics.

EFFECTIVE LEARNING SUPPORT

The research undertaken at Loughborough was part of a national research project managed by the Further Education Development Agency (FEDA) 'Differing Approaches to Effective Learning Support'. The aim of the project was to examine a range of ways in which learners were supported inside and outside the classroom. The college Curriculum Development Officer, Business Services, participated in leading an action research process piloting and evaluating a model of managed learning, using this research to produce a dissertation for her MA at Leicester University. The Deputy Head of the Faculty of Community and General Education contributed as it was his responsibility to implement good practice identified in the pilot phase. The national project aimed to help ten colleges 'to think differently about learning support, which had previously been very much part of the deficit model' and move towards considering learning support as an entitlement for all (Member of Education Staff, FEDA). The purpose of the research project in Loughborough College centred on examining the role of tutors:

> Initially we carried out research by developing a model of managed learning. We used the project to pilot the process and then gather statistics on student retention and student achievement which would either support or otherwise the model. In a sense, this project grew out of ... the perceived need to develop the tutoring process and to specifically locate tutoring within the curriculum, rather than it being just concerned with a pastoral role. We perceived the tutoring process to be seen as almost a bolted-on activity which did not really reflect the whole of the student's experience. We felt we needed to develop a pastoral role to take into account much more the academic needs of the student.... As a college we felt we needed to go in this direction, driven quite enthusiastically by the Executive who supported this all the way through.
>
> (Deputy Head of Faculty)

This research therefore focused on one of the key areas in the developing curriculum, that of managing learning, rather than managing teaching.

The leaders of the project at national level and within the college, and the Deputy Head of Faculty, were interviewed to provide different perspectives on the purpose, implementation and outcomes of the research.

The existing supportive relationship between FEDA and the college staff was part of the motivation to undertake the research. FEDA provided a framework, aiding the development of specific aims and objectives, timescale and required resources, and offering a network for mutual support with other colleges participating in the project. The commitment of the College Executive to this direction and willingness to look positively at the resulting recommendations provided additional impetus. FEDA would provide a further channel for dissemination with the possibility of the research leading to outcomes in other colleges. The base on which the research was founded was therefore both personal relationships and micropolitical commitment.

The choice of action research as an approach related to the urgent need to firstly address a specific problem. The group chosen for the pilot, Intermediate GNVQ Business, had significant problems with student achievement and retention. It was felt that if a new model of learning management could have an impact on this course, it could work with any course. A new course structure was designed through discussion by the Curriculum Development Officer, the Deputy Head of Faculty and the Director of Programmes:

> We created quite a radical structure for the course where we established a roughly 60/40 per cent unit teaching to learning management time. As a gut reaction, the College felt that it was over-teaching subjects. Because of the nature of GNVQ with many activities involved, for example integrated assignments which involve a lot of researching and coming back with information, sometimes there was a bigger need for time when the group could come together with a 'super tutor', a learning tutor, who had previously been called a personal tutor. We changed the name to stress the curriculum involvement of the tutor, a learning tutor as opposed to the previous personal tutor. The basic concept was to give the learning tutor a lot of time with the group, in some instances 6/7 hours out of the 16/17 hours that were available.
>
> (Deputy Head of Faculty)

The allocation of such a significant proportion of available time to learning management was indeed radical and a leap of faith. However, the evaluation of the process was careful and systematic:

> The pilot was evaluated at two points in the process, halfway through and then at the end of the year, when questions were asked using questionnaires to all students. A case study approach was also adopted with a group of four students which encompassed equal male and female, and ethnic mix and a student who had returned after a gap from learning. At both points of evaluation the students were interviewed and observation was made of their achievements.
>
> (Curriculum Development Officer)

The evaluation of the pilot was very positive:

- good retention (1995–96): 84 per cent completion;
- improved pass rates (1995–96) 100 per cent;
- improved grading evidence;
- good relationship between the learning tutor and student;
- good transferable skill development;
- better monitoring of progress and attendance;
- flexible model that can cope with diverse student needs (e.g. international students).

The results led to the intention to implement the new model. The process mirrored that of Rugby, in that, if an impact on the organisation was to be achieved, then conceptual, attitudinal and instrumental changes were needed. The research itself was merely the start point. The micropolitical process concerned building support amongst lecturers and managers. The former had some fears about the changes involved:

> There was some resistance to structuring time more clearly as people felt the traditional pastoral role was in danger. The evidence of the benefits to students which resulted from the pilot phase had some effect on people but not a lot. There was a sort of stigma attached to GNVQs and non-GNVQ tutors didn't understand it.
>
> (Curriculum Development Officer)

The mere logic of the results was insufficient to change staff attitudes. A process of building support began, with the research reported to the college GNVQ Council, discussion with the Principal, the Head of Student Services, and the Quality and Curriculum Manager. Cross-college meetings were also held involving representatives of different programme areas. This activity resulted in a policy document and decision to implement the model across all full-time programmes. The action research cycle was halted at this point, leading, in the view of the Curriculum Development Officer, to a missed opportunity to pilot more widely and explore the impact of the new model within 'A' level, NVQs and part-time programmes. In her view, this hiatus was caused by the sector-wide focus on operational issues, which followed incorporation:

> When curriculum development takes place piloting is needed. Colleges need to have the time to pilot, the time and space to review and adjust, and develop more than one example of good practice. The whole college approach to curriculum development at that time wasn't there. Also the sector at that time had a focus on operational issues. Colleges are now coming back to a focus on teaching and learning and moving into a more developmental role. There is more focus now on developing the curriculum.
>
> (Curriculum Development Officer)

In this instance, the capacity of the individual and the institution to build on research and develop its outcomes may be related not just to the context of the college, but also to the context of the sector as a whole. The combination of the sector-wide environment, the fears and resistance of staff, and insufficient support to faculties internally, resulted in a patchy implementation of the model in the immediate period after the pilot, but longer term consistent and coherent change is now taking place, to the benefit of students and staff:

> The benefits to students of the project have been increased confidence in their learning and ability to challenge the college and themselves. There is also evidence of higher levels of achievement amongst students. The benefits to staff have been tutors achieving a wider awareness of the whole pupil and the whole programme in which they are involved. The model encourages staff to work more closely with other teachers and therefore be more effective in meeting students' needs.
>
> (Curriculum Development Officer)

The very success of the project has raised further questions for the college, such as the responsibility for supporting staff in carrying out this very demanding multi-skilled role, and has led to cultural change:

> The project has had an impact on the culture in the college and has changed it. Where previously the single most prevalent base of resistance was a feeling 'that's all right for GNVQ' and there was no evidence to argue otherwise, now other staff feel supported by learning tutors as communication is more effective with students and there's more flexibility in the curriculum. The culture change within the college from a focus on finance to a focus on teaching and learning has been felt in a number of ways including some impact on structure.
>
> (Curriculum Development Officer)

It is evident that undertaking this research subjected the Curriculum Development Officer to additional pressures, meeting the demands of the FEDA national project, writing the dissertation and networking across the college as an addition to an already heavy commitment to teaching and management roles within the college. The benefits of the internal and external relationships were emotional as well as practical, providing moral support and valuable opportunities for networking. The fact that the research has had such a significant impact relates to the skill of the researcher in marshalling and integrating a number of personal relationships and micropolitical pressures to establish a positive force which would bolster the relatively weak force of the evidence and recommendations themselves.

TRANSFORMING THE CURRICULUM

In all the examples explored, research was essentially a part of a process of culture change to transform the curriculum to one where the support of learning was central. Mereside Sixth Form College was concerned to find a means of understanding the complexity of the learning of students, and to support staff not to be pressured into crude measures of evaluating their own or learners' performance, but to respond to the individual need of each unique learning experience. The technical college in the United Arab Emirates used research to move from a top-down system to one where those most closely aware of the needs of students could use that knowledge to inform curriculum development. Both Rugby and Loughborough Colleges were using research to power a radical shift to a proactive involvement in managing and supporting individual learning. In all cases, the research was only a partial cause of the results. The context created before and after the actual research implementation, and the building of support at several levels, was critical. Nevertheless, summarising what has been learned from these examples the research provided the opportunity for:

- growth of the researcher in conceptual understanding, practical skills and confidence;
- relationship building with colleagues internally and sector-wide;
- a systematic and rigorous process to gather evidence to support future action;
- recommendations which gave a clear plan of action;
- a catalyst for building micropolitical support for culture change.

Research alone may be a relatively weak force, but research managed by the researcher as part of a change process can be an invaluable contribution to transforming the curriculum.

5

TRANSFORMING STRUCTURES AND CULTURE

Jacky Lumby

STRUCTURAL CHANGE AND CULTURAL CHANGE

The structure of an organisation can be formally represented in a number of ways: by organisation diagrams charting the relationships and lines of communication, by job descriptions indicating role responsibility and lines of accountability, by the complex matrices outlining pay levels and job titles. The visual representations communicate one level of reality, the public statement of how people will relate to each other within the organisation. However, as O'Neill (1994a, p. 103) argues, the formal structures and processes of an organisation 'are themselves cultural artifacts' and beneath the transparent intentions, embody the values and beliefs of the school or college. The representations of structure reflect current norms and values and can be amended to reflect the direction of cultural change. Modifications in structure may also in themselves shift the norms and values of the organisation. Changes in structure may therefore both follow and foreshadow cultural change.

The overt statements of how people are to be rewarded, their role and place in the organisation, are significant indicators not only of what it is expected that each person shall do, but also of the status and value placed on each role. The organisation diagrams which represent structure are likely to be conceived in hierarchical form. O'Neill posits a widespread move to less hierarchical and bureaucratic organisations in response to the need 'to simultaneously assimilate multiple changes' (*op. cit.*, p. 114). The rate of change imposed on schools and colleges is therefore one pressure leading to structural change. The changing paradigm of teaching and learning, as explored in the chapter on curriculum in this volume, is also influencing moves to blur the previously clear distinctions between staff who teach and those who do not. In their study of associate staff, Mortimore *et al.* (1994) chart changing roles, spanning a spectrum from associate staff taking over more of the administrative and preparatory tasks, to release teachers to concentrate on teaching, to a more radical acceptance of the possibility of associate staff being involved in achieving learning. Thomas and Martin (1996, p. 163) in their study of 12 schools, also found that 'Schools are rethinking their use of support staff in terms of the direct assistance they can offer the curriculum.' A parallel metamorphosis in further education is presented by Kedney and Brownlow (1994) in Figure 5.1.

Traditional support roles	Flexible support roles
Minimum involvement with students, in support of teaching staff	More involvement, directly in support of students
Technicians and administrators	Instructors, writers, designers, workshop supervisors, etc.
Fixed blocks of time commitment during course taught hours	Flexible demands on time, spread between a number of courses
Administrative peaks and troughs (e.g. admission, assessment)	Workload more spread out (roll-on, roll-off attendance)
Fewer demands on guidance and support (because of fixed pathways through the curriculum offer)	More demands on guidance and support (flexible curriculum offer)

Figure 5.1 The role of education support staff (Kedney and Brownlow, 1994, p. 12)

The rethinking of the possible contribution of associate staff, allied to the increased use of part-time staff, has led to some uncertainties and anxieties. This is perhaps most apparent in the further education sector, where flexibility in pay and rewards and the use of part-time staff (FEDA, 1995) are greater than in schools. However, even in the relative stability of primary and secondary schools, Mortimore *et al.* (1994) note that innovations in the use of associate staff have led to tensions. The commitment of many principals to achieve a 'whole' or 'one staff' approach signals a cultural change which may be difficult to achieve.

This chapter explores the role practitioner research may play in the process, by analysis of a convenience sample of four case examples, each chosen to reflect one aspect of managing structure. In the first, Charles Keene College wished to review its pay and reward structure. In William Shrewsbury Primary and Summerhill Secondary schools, the researchers aimed to contribute to the more effective use of associate staff. In the final case of a secondary school, the Head of Music wished to explore the integration of peripatetic staff and those part-time staff who were based permanently in the school. In this case a pseudonym is used, Bowen Secondary School. Each example is of course unique, and illustrates different aspects of the possible role of practitioner research.

DEVELOPING PAY AND REWARD MECHANISMS

The demise of national pay structures in the further education sector since incorporation in 1993 has led to a proliferation of different approaches to pay and reward mechanisms. The high staffing costs, typically 75–80 per cent of all operating costs (Brain, 1994) has rendered the efficient and effective management of staff of great importance. There have also been sector-wide concerns that current pay and reward mechanisms may not be achieving the desired outcome of encouraging excellent performance, teamwork and innovation:

> While managers may claim to want staff with initiative and creativity, they may actually be rewarding conformity; where they claim to stress the importance of teaching and learning skills or of experience, they are rewarding those with degrees and higher qualifications; while they aim to create teams of equals, those same teams contain staff on a multitude of grades.
>
> (Brain, 1994, p. 91)

The incongruence of intentions and action is experienced in the context of a changing sector, where the increasing appointment of non-education-alists with specialist skills has further complicated the issue by compelling the consideration of pay and reward mechanisms used to attract and retain staff outside education. These concerns were considered by senior staff at Charles Keene College. There was a wish to investigate more effective ways of encouraging and rewarding individual perfor-mance. The Personnel Manager aimed to achieve a pay and reward policy and used the dissertation of his MBA with Leicester University to forward this aim. The Personnel Manager and the Head of the Faculty of

Administration were interviewed to assess the impact of the work on the individual and on the college.

Senior management were enrolled in support of the work from the start as the Director of Personnel circulated a brief paper outlining his intentions and discussed his ideas with the Head of the Faculty of Administration. It was agreed that this was a sensitive area, but one which it would be useful to pursue. The Personnel Manager wished to build his own personal knowledge of the different approaches in the sector for self-development, but also to ensure that a level of expertise and innovative ideas were available within the college which could enrich internal discussions. Early in the work, in the words of the Head of Faculty, 'real life intervened' in the shape of a proposed merger with another college. This obviously meant that pay and reward mechanisms would be very much under discussion in terms of harmonisation of conditions if the merger went ahead, but it also elongated the time scale as the decision on whether the merger was to proceed would be needed before definitive decisions could be taken.

A survey by questionnaire of all colleges in England and Wales was undertaken as well as semi-structured interviews with Charles Keene staff. The interviews allowed the issues to be discussed in depth and with sensitivity. The college was supportive in trusting the Personnel Manager to implement a national survey and providing the resource to produce and distribute the questionnaires, collate the results and return a summary report to respondents. The results were discussed with colleagues on an ongoing basis, though the Personnel Manager was realistic about the amount of time that senior staff could give to supporting the work.

The Personnel Manager felt that he had achieved many benefits from the process. Apart from increasing the skills involved in the discipline of research, there was the sense of performing a task well in a way which otherwise might not have happened:

> The research was structured in such a way that it was a very methodical and disciplined way of working. It would have been very easy to have not done it in the sort of detail that the dissertation required and that was invaluable, to sit down with individuals and to say 'I need half an hour of your time to be able to talk through these issues', giving the reason as the dissertation. The research project enabled discussions to take place, and views to be sought and feelings recorded, that wouldn't have been done properly otherwise.

The links established with other colleges also proved fruitful, initiating an ongoing dialogue. The growth in expertise also increased the personal credibility of the Personnel Manager, of use in career terms at a time when the value of managers is under scrutiny due to the potential merger.

The impact on the organisation was seen as long term. There was no doubt that the process was seen as one of 'changing culture' (Personnel Manager) and that the research to date had provided the foundation for further discussion: 'I think this is the start of a lot more work' (Personnel Manager). The time scale was projected as about a year, with the development of the policy built into the academic year's action plan:

> I think it will enable the college to be more confident in developing a policy and strategy for the future, and hopefully they'll have more confidence in me to be able to do that, having done this research.
>
> (Personnel Manager)

The Head of the Faculty of Administration was clear that the research had revealed that there was no definitive answer to an appropriate pay and reward system, and the follow up process would involve micropolitical negotiations, where some of the innovative ideas suggested through the research would need to be suggested with care. The unforeseen element of the potential merger might give additional impetus as a new system would have to be agreed. From his perspective, the potential outcomes of research are partly dependant on selecting an area which is strategically aligned with the direction of senior management, and partly luck:

> It's the benefit of choosing the right subject at the right time, and then to a degree it's a question of luck, being in the right place at the right time and in such a way that you can actually implement. So there are a number of factors which have got to come together. You have then got to have the support of the Chief Executive of the organisation, who has to feel that that is a good thing, that that is what we wanted and now we are going to implement it.

A new pay and reward mechanism may well have been agreed anyway, but the research has given the college a more solid foundation on which to build; without it, the Personnel Manager felt 'I'm not sure we would have done it so well'.

ACHIEVING ONE STAFF IN A PRIMARY SCHOOL

William Shrewsbury is a large primary school with a village catchment on the Northern fringe of Burton-on-Trent. An increase in both the number of non-teaching staff employed and the hours worked per week led the Head of the infant section of the school, then undertaking an MBA at Leicester University, to research the process of their selection, recruitment and induction. However, the underlying theme of the research was to explore the current perceptions of all staff on the role of non-teaching staff and to increase the effectiveness of the latter's role. The research involved interviews with a range of staff and concluded by recommending a number of changes to the recruitment, selection, induction and staff development processes for non-teaching staff. To investigate the impact of this work, the Head of Infants, the Ancillary Assistant for Reception and Nursery, and the Headteacher were interviewed, thus providing a number of perspectives on how the practitioner research was received and its impact.

The Head of Infants explained that as she commenced her research, the recruitment and selection process was very *ad hoc*, selecting 'Mrs So and So on the playground who could come and do ten hours a week'. She also felt that there might be a need to enhance the role of non-teaching staff and involve them more in the management of learning in the classroom, so that they could become involved in the cycle of curriculum planning, assessment and evaluation, becoming 'part of the school staff'. There was a sense that they could give more, if encouraged to do so, and that the children's learning could benefit. As the research developed, it became clear that there was a cultural issue in the value assigned to non-teaching staff:

> There was very much a 'them and us' situation between the teaching staff and non-teaching staff. It varied and it's difficult to generalise. A lot of the teaching staff felt that the non-teaching staff were not trained, that they came and often did quite menial tasks directed by whatever the teachers told them to do and they didn't ask much from them. The non-teaching staff themselves felt that they couldn't do much. They were quite in awe of the teachers and quite frightened to ask things or to volunteer suggestions on ways of doing things in the classroom which might have been good and valid suggestions. So it was trying to change a whole attitude so that non-teaching staff were part of the staff team and not just people who came in, washed up the paint pots and went home again.
>
> (Head of Infants)

The research was therefore focused on one level on the practical processes of recruitment and development of staff, but on another level was addressing the fundamental structure of staff within the school. There were also personal aims, in that the Head of Infants wished to improve her understanding of the perspectives of all staff and be more knowledgeable about recruitment, selection and induction processes.

The method chosen for the research related strongly to the personal aims. The Head of Infants felt that there was little opportunity to talk to non-teaching staff about how they felt about their role. Any changes that the research suggested would need the support of teaching staff and therefore it was important to talk through their perceptions and needs with them. Consequently a survey was conducted using semi-structured interviews, allowing some probing into people's perceptions and attitudes.

During the period in which the research was carried out there were a number of staff changes. The Headteacher who was in post at the start of the research was succeeded by an Acting Head. A new Headteacher was then appointed after the research had been completed. On appointment the new Head, talking to the Head of Infants, outlined his wish to achieve a 'whole school staff approach' and at this point learned of the research which had taken place. The focus of the research was very much in key with the thinking of the new Headteacher, and this played a large part in the impact of the research. From that time on, there was ongoing discussion considering the issues that the research had raised.

In personal terms, the outcomes of the research were that the Head of Infants felt more informed of how staff felt about their roles and about each other, and more knowledgeable about the processes she had investigated. It offered her an opportunity to gain insights into:

> processes and structures and what's going on at grass root level of the organisation in a way you don't always have the opportunity to explore when you're in a classroom with lots of children tearing round.

There were many instrumental outcomes for the school. There is now a formal recruitment and selection process for non-teaching staff, an induction process with a checklist of information and a guiding mentor, and a review system linked to development opportunities:

> Our policy statement and our development planning, the involvement of staff, trying to give the whole staff opportunities for their own personal and professional development ... was a direct outcome of the agenda that was set by that piece of research.
>
> (The Headteacher)

The changes permeated further than the recruitment, induction and staff development processes, in response to a number of questions that emerged from the interviews with staff:

> People expressed how they felt or didn't feel part of things, sometimes very simple things like not having a pigeon-hole. Why did some people have a pigeon-hole and not others? ... Why don't we have the weekly diary? Why don't we know what's going on? We're not told. The use of the term 'non-teaching staff'. All these things were very practical issues, some of which we could do something about straight away. There were many things that we had to deal with and are still dealing with.
>
> (The Headteacher)

As well as receiving the weekly diary, non-teaching staff were also invited to weekly planning meetings and staff development events.

The results of the changes introduced were evident in the experience of the Ancillary Assistant. Her appointment had been part of a rigorous selection process. She described the interview as 'the hardest one I have ever had', yet she did not feel that this was uncomfortable or inappropriate. On the contrary, she felt that the interview really probed her attitude to children and encouraged full and honest answers. From that point on she was fully involved in the school, invited to parents' meetings, setting up the classroom for September, and when term opened, being involved in planning and staff development. The feeling of being part of a team was strong:

> I was involved in all the planning meetings as well so that I know on a week-to-week basis what we're doing during the week. It's not like the teachers just say. I'm really involved in the planning ... I would say that all the teachers I've worked with, the approach is the same. I don't think they've got the approach that I'm doing this and you'll do that. They're not like that. It is good teamwork.
>
> (Ancillary Assistant)

In her view, the rigour of the selection process had given her confidence that she was suited to the job and wanted. The involvement in planning and support of her development had an impact. If she took circle time or was involved in other activities, she knew their purpose and could contribute. As a result, 'It's the children who benefit'.

Carrying out the research was not always easy. Interviewing associate staff depended on their good will, and finding a quiet spot in a busy school was difficult. There were interruptions from children and parents to contend with. Despite this, the research was completed and did have an impact on the individual and on the school. Several circumstances made this possible. The Head of Infants was also Professional Development Co-ordinator, and holding the formal responsibly for staff development was useful for forwarding the recommendations. The Head of Infants was indefatigable in communicating the results of her work to the Head, the Governors and other staff. The quality of the research impressed. Most importantly, the Headteacher was eager to use the work to contribute towards achieving the guiding vision of a school where all were valued. He was aware of how easy it is to remain at the level of rhetoric when considering a 'one staff' approach:

> When you introduce the idea that we are all one staff, everyone goes 'Oh yes. of course' ... You might think that you are treating everyone the same way. You might think that people take on board this idea of a whole staff but in practice it's not necessarily so, and how people themselves see it, the dinner ladies, the assistants, welfare workers, they see it in a very different way.
>
> (The Headteacher)

In his view the research allowed the school to understand better the perspective of the associate staff. The instrumental changes recommended and implemented as a result of the research undoubtedly also under-pinned conceptual change, as defined by Huberman (1993), and cultural change (O'Neill, 1994a).

It's very difficult to put down suggestions as to how you would change the culture of an organisation apart from implementing some practical things that may well begin to influence the culture. Really they were mostly practical outcomes which I hoped would have an impact on the culture of the organisation, not directly but indirectly.

(Head of Infants)

The result of the practical steps suggested was a change in status of the associate staff:

I think they didn't feel particularly valued at the beginning. I hope they feel more valued now.

Both the Head of Infants and the Headteacher felt that given the vision of the latter, the changes might have happened anyway over time, but the Headteacher saw the research as a tremendous help:

It's helped me as the Headteacher. It's given a tremendous impetus. I felt the support from the research and from her attitude and what she learned from it, so in terms of helping me develop those initiatives, the particular way of working, it's been a tremendous boost ... it's so dovetailed with what we're trying to do, so central to a great deal of how the school is developing. It's not an appendage. It's not something out there. She talks to me about her research, I talk to her about it. We relate it directly to our Development Plan and to the people who are working here so it's a living thing. It's not a bookish thing that's being carried out in a library or on a computer in her home. It's very much to do with what is happening at this moment in time.

The quality of research and determination of the researcher, the partnership between the researcher and the Headteacher, the support of other staff and governors all created a synergy whereby one small-scale piece of research has impelled the speed of change in the direction of a school which is genuinely striving to have 'one staff'.

ACHIEVING ONE STAFF IN A SECONDARY SCHOOL

Summerhill School is a secondary school in Kingswinford in the West Midlands. The research reported here has many parallels with that undertaken in William Shrewsbury School. The researcher was at the time Head of the Languages and Business Faculty. He has since moved to become an LEA Advisor/Inspector. While at Summerhill, he was interested in how far the associate staff, about a quarter of the full staff complement, were integrated into the structure and culture of the school. He was also concerned that they might not be adequately valued by staff and students. This concern was shared by the Senior Administrative Officer, who had responsibility for managing associate staff:

One of my personal concerns is that education generally doesn't necessarily see the value of associate staff within their establishment. I think there is very much still a 'them and us' situation and anything that could raise their profile and show where areas of development could take place, to me, was a very good exercise.

(Senior Administrative Officer)

A new Headteacher was appointed two months after the research was completed and began to work with the Head of Faculty and Senior Administrative Officer to make use of the research that had been done. All three people were interviewed to explore how they worked together both during and after the research period and what the impact of their joint efforts has been.

In his role as Head of the Languages and Business Faculty, the researcher had relatively little direct contact with associate, or as they were then termed, non-teaching staff. One of his personal objectives was to extend his understanding of the role of associate staff, 'to try to open up my awareness of all the people involved in the school'. He also wished to improve the way this group of staff was perceived by teachers, thereby improving their status. The method of research chosen, a survey by questionnaire and interview, allowed him to introduce himself to associate staff by handing out the questionnaires with a personal explanation. Their response impressed him. In comparison with the relatively low response rate of teachers to staff development surveys, the associate staff responded very positively. Twenty out of 21 returned the questionnaire and 17 agreed to be interviewed:

They were so favourable, so professional, that the contact developed personal relationships as well as helping the research ... People who had never met me were doing this survey as a favour to me. I asked would you mind giving up half an hour to help me with some research, and they all came back, every one ... A number of them said to me, nobody has ever asked us things like this before. Nobody has ever bothered to ask the opinion of a Lunchtime Supervisor who's on the premises for an hour-and-a-half each day.

(Head of Faculty)

The Senior Administrative Officer was also very helpful in liaising with associate staff, introducing the questionnaire to some and identifying the appropriate sample to interview. The new Headteacher was delighted to read the research and from that time on was very supportive. The interest and enthusiasm of all these people provided an incentive to the researcher, making him feel an obligation to ensure that there were results for the school as so many had given time and thought to support the research and implement its recommendations.

There have been a number of tangible outcomes from the research. The term non-teaching staff has been dropped in favour of associate staff, so that this group of staff are no longer defined by what they do not do. A Development Review process has been established to identify development needs, as the Headteacher sees it, building on the parallel process for teachers by eliminating the weaknesses of the teacher appraisal process. Though associate staff formed a quarter of the school staff, they had no representation on the governing body. Through discussion and negotiation with the governors, an elected member of associate staff has been co-opted. The role of the Senior Administrative Officer is reviewed annually. She is a full member of the Senior Management Team. The representation of associate staff on the governing body and the inclusion of the Senior Administrative Officer on the SMT are fairly rare in schools. Both actions send strong messages about the value placed on associate staff.

The role of associate staff has also been explored and developed, at both ends of the spectrum described by Mortimore *et al.* (1994). At the level of taking on more tasks that teachers do not need to do, associate staff are working directly to Heads of Department and Faculty, undertaking a wider range of administrative tasks:

> We've tried very much to link them with particular roles, areas or departments of the school, so that they can be seen to be directly supporting a subject or a year group, so their worth to the team of teachers is seen much more directly and not just as a background function.
>
> (The Headteacher)

At the other end of the spectrum, the possibility of associate staff becoming more involved in supporting teaching and learning is being discussed, not just as technicians in science, but also in other areas:

> We are having discussions as to how associate staff can help alongside teaching staff, going into classrooms, perhaps sitting alongside somebody there, a teacher nervous about using IT and supporting that role. We have already started to discuss those sorts of implications.
>
> (Senior Administrative Officer)

The sensitivity of such development is recognised and progress is to be achieved with patience and caution, taking account of the need to protect the professional role of teachers:

> It is in its very early days and so there still is quite an entrenchment of what people think their job is and therefore how other people perceive it, and once you move out of that I think you have to proceed very carefully, depending on individual relationships. I do really think that the revolution that's going to happen with ICT in schools, in some schools more quickly than others, is going to make such a huge difference to the role of teachers that we mustn't lose sight of the role of non-teachers and how we can all pull together, because we are all going to be looking at different ways of working. I think teachers hanging on preciously to certain things is not going to serve them well.
>
> (The Headteacher)

Just as in William Shrewsbury school, where tangible changes led to conceptual and attitudinal change, at Summerhill all three of those interviewed were convinced that the signals of how much associate staff were valued, the change in title, the representation on governors, the seniority of their line manager, their more direct involvement in supporting teachers, had resulted in an improvement in status. The cultural change is indicated by small signs such as the greater use of the staff room by the associate staff. Relationships have changed to the benefit of the school.

The researcher worked well in partnership with the Senior Administrative Officer and the Headteacher. His emphatic communication of the results and their implications was an important factor in convincing the governors of the need to consider change. The Headteacher was already committed to moving in the suggested direction, but things moved faster because of the research and its follow-up.

> I don't think it would have happened in quite such a focused way and so quickly; it was on my priority list but it wouldn't have come up as quickly. Because the research was helpful, useful and could just be implemented, it actually happened. It saved a lot of time on my behalf of perhaps researching, evaluating and moving forward. I would like to think that even if the research hadn't been done, we would have been thinking about it in school anyway ... but I don't think it would have happened as quickly.
>
> (The Headteacher)

The Senior Administrative Officer felt that certain things might not have happened without the research, such as representation on the governing body. There was certainly an impact, and in common with other examples in this volume, the impact was due to the individual efforts of the researcher and the support of senior staff. The element which is perhaps particularly notable in this example, is that the associate staff themselves, by the quality of their response, their ideas and enthusiasm, succeeded in contributing to a commitment on the part of the researcher to ensure that the research would achieve what it set out to do. It is not only the support of senior staff that can make a difference.

INTEGRATING PART-TIME STAFF

The final example in this chapter focuses on a Head of Music who was the only full-time member of his department. Other staff comprised a member of teaching staff, and an Administrative Assistant, both of whom were full-time in the school, but only part-time in the department, and a number of peripatetic staff who might be in the school every day or for only half an hour a week. He suspected that particularly the peripatetic staff might not feel fully part of the department and that their teaching might not be integrated in the bigger picture of the department curriculum. He sought to use research to explore how a policy of integration might be achieved. The Head of Music, the Administrative Assistant and a peripatetic teacher were interviewed to investigate different perspectives on the impact of this research.

The Head of Music had undertaken previous research as part of his MBA with Leicester University. He felt that perhaps he had tried to cover too much, involving too many people and a tighter focus might be more manageable. There had also been little support from senior managers and so it seemed that recommendations which related to the department, and which therefore he could implement, might be more appropriate. He felt that some peripatetic staff who had come into the school for some years, and were in more frequently each week, were comfortable with the arrangement. However, others, such as the teacher of the tabla, might 'walk in, do 40 minutes teaching and walk out again without even a cup of coffee'. This concern was shared by both the peripatetic teacher and the Administrative Assistant. The former felt that there was a relationship between the feeling of belonging and the teaching that took place. If staff felt 'strange and very lonely' then:

> of course that has an impact on the way you teach. I feel that students mirror your feelings. If you feel down, then you're not going to get the best out of a student. They will pick it up from you.

The problem was that nobody was likely to spot when peripatetic staff had problems:

> Many peripatetic staff do get depressed. If there are personal problems nobody knows.

The Administrative Assistant felt that some peripatetic staff made an effort and tried to get to know others in the school. Others couldn't because of time restrictions, or seemed unwilling to try. The Head of Music believed that there was a need to integrate full-time staff who worked part-time in the department, but that the problems of integrating peripatetic staff were more intransigent. He wanted to confirm or otherwise his belief that a greater degree of integration was needed to support individuals in the department, but also to ensure that their teaching was seen as part of the whole:

> I was hoping that out of it would come a greater understanding from the peripatetic staff that the students they're teaching, the work they're doing is part of an examination, rather than, I just come in and teach the clarinet. It's part of a bigger picture. I don't know whether I've got that across yet.

The issues to be addressed by the research were therefore at the farthest end of the spectrum of difficulty caused by the changing nature of employment in education. The difficulties encountered by those managing growing numbers of part-time or contract staff are seen in extreme form by this Head of Music attempting to create a structure to support and integrate teachers employed by an agency and in school for perhaps a very small amount of time.

The research was carried out in difficult circumstances. A survey by questionnaire was chosen so that the Head of Music could spot a peripatetic member of staff leaving, dash out of class to give a quick explanation and hand over the questionnaire. As it was just before Christmas all the peripatetic staff were very busy with concerts. Interviewing the other music teacher and the Administrative Assistant was easier. No support was given from outside the department.

The outcomes of the research were limited. In personal terms, the research provided a vehicle to talk to staff and to better understand their experience of working in the department. The resulting recommendations included:

- the publication of a half-termly bulletin to inform staff of developments and events;
- the publication of the Head of Department's timetable so that staff would know when he was free;
- amending the part-time teacher's timetable to ensure whole groups were taught, not just shared groups;
- better management of the Administrative Assistant's tasks;
- providing restroom, noticeboard and refreshment facilities;
- involving everybody more in extra curricular activities.

For a number of reasons, none of these things happened. Circumstances converged to rob the Head of Music of the personal and professional commitment to persist. Firstly, immediately after Christmas the whole school was 'plunged into an OFSTED inspection' (Head of Music). The inspection gave the department a good report. At the same time a number of personal problems entered the life of the Head of Music, changing his focus:

> When I was doing this I was a lot more switched on. A number of personal issues have come to the fore in my life and have taken precedence for the moment. I've been here for seven years and I can afford not to keep pushing and pushing. Things will get done. I didn't do anything differently for OFSTED and OFSTED said I was a good teacher, so while I'm trying to sort these personal issues out, and they are getting sorted, the whole school thing is in the background.

(Head of Music)

Part of the context appears to be an effective Head of Department, who was thought highly of by the Administrative Assistant and the peripatetic teacher, with therefore no urgent incentive to change. Given the absence of anybody motivating him from elsewhere in the school, the personal problems understandably tipped the balance away from the persistence and commitment needed to ensure that research bears fruit.

Setting aside the personal and practical difficulties encountered, there may also have been a problem with the research aims. The peripatetic teacher was quite sceptical of schools' ability to tackle the issue of integrating staff. She felt that it would be 'wonderful' if schools took on some of the role of supporting peripatetic staff but:

> I think it's very hard for schools because they haven't got a lot of time. Visiting peripatetic teachers are just something extra. I don't think they would have time to do that. It's up to peripatetic teachers to do it themselves.

The increasing demands on schools may mean that they are forced to deal with only core activities, passing on what responsibilities they can to others, including that of managing the peripatetic service. In her view, the responsibility lay with the agency who employed peripatetic staff, but financial exigencies meant that there was little room for manoeuvre.

The recommendations themselves were seen by the Head of Music as perhaps 'a bit simplistic'. The publishing of his timetable would not help staff who were only in the department at times when he was not free. The cost of involving peripatetic staff more in extra curricular work was prohibitive. Nevertheless, there were a number of ideas which could have helped provide a greater degree of cement in the department, and the Head of Music was recovering from a very difficult period to consider moving on and perhaps trying to implement his ideas.

> At the moment I feel, yeah, yeah, about life in general, but thinking about the way I feel now compared to six weeks, two months ago, when I just wanted to leave teaching, I feel a lot more positive now, so if that continues then I might go back to this work. It's not a no. It's not ruled out.

This example shows a practitioner researcher who selected a particularly difficult management issue and achieved little impact because of a combination of in-school and out-of-school circumstances. However, at what point should the impact of research be measured? It may be that the insight provided by this work will influence the management style and practice of the researcher in the future. It may be that in six months time, the motivation and energy to continue will have returned and outcomes will be visible. In this sense it is difficult to choose a moment in time at which to judge the outcome of research. Balancing this more positive view may be the argument that the issues to be addressed were insoluble and that integrating a teacher who appears for only half an hour a week when the Head of Department is not free is not within the bounds of possibility. The final judgement probably lies somewhere between the two. Plans were in place to implement some of the more straightforward recommendations, but even if implemented, there is likely to be a small rather than a significant impact on so difficult an issue. Should research therefore select issues which are capable of solution, or should practitioners engage in research which runs a risk of being sterile, but may impact in a small way on the lives of individual teachers, and through them on the students? Certainly the chief lesson from this case example was that the responsibility for the outcomes of the research were shouldered firmly by the Head of Music:

> Things would have happened if I had rattled the cage enough. The onus is on me rather than the institution.

Having seen examples of where partnership was the key to results, this example illustrates a researcher acting autonomously. The question is how far the limited results relate to personal circumstances, leading to odds stacked too high against the researcher for results in the short-term, to the lack of support from outside the department or to the inherent difficulties of the problems addressed.

TRANSFORMING STRUCTURES

The four case examples explored illustrate that practitioner research can contribute to the development of structures and culture in schools and colleges. The power of partnerships, particularly with the Headteacher and senior management is clear, but the support of others, such as associate staff, can be an important element. The individual motivation of the researcher is vital, as the carrying out and writing up of research is merely the initial stage. The impact demonstrated in this chapter depended on the energy and determination of the practitioner to disseminate, involve, convince and bring about practical change. As the Head of Infants pointed out, it is through sometimes small practical changes, that cultural change happens. It is no coincidence that the most common definition of culture is 'the way we *do* things around here' (my italics) (Bush, 1995, pp. 132–3). In all the cases the time scale was lengthy. Indeed, as in the final case, it is impossible to measure the impact of research in any definitive sense, in that the work may continue to influence personal style and actions and events for many years to come. Research may provide the context and confidence for further work, as in Charles Keene College, or may lead to immediate tangible results, such as the associate staff representation on the governing body at Summerhill. Its success in having an impact on the organisation relates to two sets of ingredients, those brought by the researcher and those brought by the organisation. The former brings his or her micropolitical sensitivity in choosing the right focus, enlisting support, carrying out the research well and above all, pursuing the implementation of what is learned. The organisation provides guidance in the choice of focus, support while the research is carried out, and commitment to making use of the lessons. Where these two sets of conditions come together, then significant instrumental, conceptual and cultural change can result.

SECTION B:
AFFECTING THE SCHOOL
AS AN INSTITUTION

6

SOME EFFECTS OF MULTIPLE RESEARCH PROJECTS ON THE HOST SCHOOL STAFF AND THEIR RELATIONSHIPS

David Middlewood

INTRODUCTION

This chapter examines some of the effects that occur when a number of research projects are carried out in one school, either by several people being involved in one or more projects, or by a single person doing several separate projects. From the wide experience of the authors of this book and analysis of the many pieces of research undertaken in these contexts, the effects upon the school are seen to be primarily in the broad area of the people within it. This is hardly surprising since schools 'are people centred because young people are at the heart of their business' (Bush and Middlewood, 1997, p. viii). Since schools and their effectiveness depend upon the quality of the people who work there, and the relationships between them, this chapter focuses upon those two areas. What are the effects of multiple research upon the staff as individuals and upon their relationships within the school? The latter question of course includes the fundamental relationship of staff and students. If research does not ultimately lead to some improvement for the most important people, the pupils/students, then its merit has to be questioned. Since the research projects in question concern themselves with management, then the effects sought will be improvement in the management of all people since 'Sensitive management of people as individuals with different personalities, backgrounds and personal and professional needs is a vital dimension in the development of successful organisations' (*ibid.*, p. ix).

METHODOLOGY

Fourteen different schools in England in which several staff were engaged in accredited research assignments were used. A questionnaire concerning the effects of the research work was sent to the 107 teachers and 72 completed ones were received (a 67 per cent response rate) from across those schools. The numbers involved in the individual schools concerned ranged from 16 to two. The author had been involved in a tutorial role with each of the schools at some stage of their work, although the extent of the involvement varied considerably. It had been possible to hold semi-structured interviews with the researchers and with school managers at various stages therefore. Additionally, such interviews were held with managers or research programme co-ordinators at six different schools during the spring and summer terms of 1998. In two schools from which questionnaires were received no interviews were possible and in three schools (see Chapter 7) more than one manager was interviewed. This is summarised in Table 6.1.

Table 6.1 *Numbers of staff involved in research*

Schools	No. of staff involved	No. of staff returning questionnaire	No. of staff interviewed at least once	No. of managers interviewed in 1998
A	16	14	12	3
B	12	10	9	2
C	11	8	8	2
D	10	6	8	1
E	10	7	7	1
F	10	8	8	0
G	9	5	6	1
H	8	4	5	0
I	6	4	5	0
J	5	3	4	0
K	3	2	3	0
L	3	0	2	0
M	2	0	0	0
N	2	1	0	0
Totals	**107**	**72**	**77**	**10**

EFFECTS UPON STAFF AS INDIVIDUALS

(a) In Terms of Personal and Career Development

In arguing for personal development programmes for teachers, Waters (1998) makes the point that it is important for teachers to discover any untapped potential, as well as, possibly, valuable transferable skills. This, he argues, is empowering and, if it means a few such empowered teachers leave the profession, this is worth it because their potential will be fulfilled elsewhere. Day (1996) has also argued that teachers' lives and personal development are central to an understanding of their potential for development as professionals. One of the findings from the individual teachers' comments was the almost universal (90 per cent of respondents) 'untapping' of the ability 'to be a researcher' that was revealed.

> I didn't know I could do it; now I know I can
>
> (Stuart, Warwickshire school)
>
> I thought research was something done by professors, now I know I'm a researcher!
>
> (Jane, Leicester school)

Overwhelmingly (94 per cent of respondents), teachers felt that they had learned new skills which were relevant and which boosted their professional standing. The importance of sustained research in enabling the refinement of these new skills was stressed by a teacher.

> We've had a one-off research project – funded by the TTA [Teacher Training Agency] – and that was helpful. But only when I did my third and fourth pieces of research, did I feel I was getting it just right. Like everything else, you get better and better by practising the skill. Doing research is the same.
>
> (Anon., Northampton school)

An example of this may lie in a tendency in the first piece of research to be pre-determined upon a particular methodology, i.e. knowing what you're going to investigate and deciding at the same time, for example, to send out a questionnaire. Only with tutorial help and experience did teachers realise that the vital point was to ask:

• What do I need to know and why? Only then do you ask 'What is the best way to collect information' and 'When I have this information, what shall I do with it?' as advised by Bell (1987, p.50).

This actual skill as a researcher (the process), linked with the extensive additional knowledge generated by the research (outcome), was directly responsible according to a number of teachers (52.6 per cent) for advancing their professional careers, either through promotion to a more senior post in another school or within their current school. In one school, for example, of the seven teachers involved in research, six were internally promoted and the other gained promotion elsewhere. Teachers attributed this to their greater understanding of such things as decision-making processes, understanding of the importance of people's feelings and views, the recognition of the centrality of the student. Furthermore, the actual engagement in research was evidence of a commitment to school improvement, and teachers reported that at selection interviews they were able to give answers grounded in evidence.

> I was not only able to say I had achieved something successful, but I could show why I knew it was successful.
>
> (Mike, Leicester school)

The headteacher of the school where the internal promotions had been made, mentioned above, said:

> Frankly, those who were doing the research wiped the floor with the rest. They knew so much about the school, much that I didn't, that their arguments were powerful. Where we didn't agree, the debate was what you'd want to have with the person appointed anyway.

On a most practical level, Jo Fl (Corby school) said:

> So much wisdom has been accumulated now. Frankly, if I were called for interview and got the job details, the first thing I'd do is consult our set of assignments as a reference – someone will have done something. I mean that genuinely.

Moyra (Leicester school):

> My confidence in preparation for answering at interviews is increased. I can speak more authoritatively now and if I don't know, I'll say I know what I'd do to find out.

(b) In Terms of Being Reflective Practitioners

Hoyle and McCormick's (1976) model of extended professionality includes a number of elements relevant here, e.g. high in involvement in professional activities (e.g. research), regular reading of professional literature, value placed on professional collaboration. These were features of the effects on themselves to which the vast majority of teachers referred. 'Getting beneath the surface', 'Finding out the real situation', 'Gave me greater insight' were phrases that were used regularly by teachers reporting upon how their own research into school practice enabled them to reflect upon the teaching, management and all the work done by themselves and colleagues in school. Sue (Clacton school) said she had found it:

> fascinating to get behind the exterior gloss and find out what people really felt and the processes that were really happening, rather than the appearances that were given.

She went on to say how she now no longer made automatic assumptions about student or staff reactions but 'reflected' on what they might mean or why they occurred. David (Leicester school) said:

> it has helped me to analyse change, by standing back and reflecting on what I'm doing.

Ros (Leicester school) believed she was better able to assess her own and others' actual techniques through having researched learning styles.

Contributing to teachers' increased reflectiveness upon practice, indeed inextricably linked with it, is the researchers' involvement in reading. Reading was highlighted by 60 per cent of the teachers as being (a) something which had been 'rediscovered' (b) something which they found interesting and (c) something which they could not now stop! Twenty per cent of the teachers in fact, when asked about problems, reported that restricting the reading was a major difficulty:

> I just get so interested in so many things, it was hard to restrict myself to what was relevant to my own research.
>
> (Judy, Bedfordshire school)

Kate (Bedfordshire school) memorably described her new habitual reading as being noted for 'ah-hah' moments, meaning I would read that and say "Ah-hah! I could do that at school." ' This tendency to take the reading more widely than anticipated is probably however relevant to an aspect of the effects of research mentioned by 70 per cent of teachers, namely the increased sharing through informal discussion. The link lies in the fact that the reading not being restricted to a narrow field of focus no doubt helped the conversations between teachers where topics discussed would overlap. In any case, talking and 'gossiping' with other colleagues about, initially, each other's research and later educational issues in general, was clearly a widespread and powerful outcome of in-house practitioner research.

> We had always nattered non-stop, and mostly about the children – along with the news, television and the lottery! I realised after a while we were still talking non-stop about the children, but it was much more about *why* people did things, whether it could be done a better way, do you think it's because so-and-so, relating to something we'd read or had in a lecture. Colleagues will say on a topic someone raises 'I was reading the other day that that might be because ...' Once, we'd always say 'Oh, they've been on a course!' Now, we just all join in! And it's not just those doing the research, it's the others too. They'll say to us 'Have you looked into that?' or 'Have you come across anything on this?'
>
> (Jenny, Wellingborough School)

Not only does this shared discussion illustrate Hoyle and McCormick's 'professional collaboration' but it fits with the more recent notion of a 'collaborative culture' in schools (Fullan and Hargreaves, 1992) and the firm belief of researchers such as Hopkins and Lagerweij (1996, p. 87) 'that one of the characteristics of successful schools is that *teachers talk about teaching*'. Since they also stress that 'we have for too long been content with anecdotal evidence and perceptual data collected unsystematically' (*ibid.*, p. 88), that the focus of the talk should be teachers' own research must be a powerful aid to school improvement.

EFFECTS UPON RELATIONSHIPS IN SCHOOLS

Schools, as people-centred organisations with a central purpose of effective learning and teaching which is characterised by effective relationships, are inevitably heavily dependent upon the quality of the relationships. Lofthouse (1994, p.132) describes the first two features of a 'culture of integration' as:

> strong personal relationships (e.g. social interaction and cohersion) strong professional relationships (e.g. task related working parties, curriculum leaders, paired teaching).

From the responses of the teachers and managers in the schools studied, one of the significant areas influenced by the existence of a research group was that of relationships, between various people. For convenience, they are sub-divided as follows: relationships between staff and students, between staff, and between senior managers and teachers.

(a) Relationships between Teachers and Students

The central relationship in any school or college must be that of teachers and their students and this relationship appeared to have been affected through teachers carrying out research in three ways:

(i) by *what* they found out about students i.e. knowledge obtained through content of the investigation;

(ii) by what they found out from doing research *with* the students i.e. understanding of students through the process and;

(iii) what they found out by *being* students themselves i.e. identifying through emphasising.

(i) The first of these, where the content of the particular piece of research directly involved students, is best dealt with in Chapter 8 'Engendering Change', because these concern themselves more with specific research assignments. One or two points may be made here, however. The first is that it is surprisingly recent that in the educational system generally we have begun asking the immediate 'customers' what they think of the service they are receiving. As Holland (1998) points out, the practice is widespread in other services and, in his view, will become one of the huge features of learning in the 21st century. The second is that most teachers quickly discovered that researching directly into student work was very enjoyable. In one sense, as 60 per cent of respondents noted, students provide the most accessible means of data to be gathered – they are 'captive' (the word commonly used). A high response rate can be guaranteed with a class in front of you! Additionally, however, teachers found that investigating a topic such as 'boys and modern languages', or 'self-esteem', 'under-achievement in Year 8' or 'independent learning in the sixth form', for example, is likely to remain remotely theoretical unless the students concerned are asked for their views or perceptions. Not only such views, but, for example, students keeping records of use of private study or homework can and did provide valuable primary data for teacher researchers.

(ii) However, some of the above category may still be seen as in the context of the 'teacher in control' relationship. Indeed, with 30 students being asked to complete some questions for the teacher, it may be inevitable. More interesting in its effects upon staff/student relationships is what several teachers described as revealing through the *process* of student involvement. Three examples may illustrate the point.

Tina (librarian in Northamptonshire school) did a research assignment on the management of the library in terms of curriculum support at 16 plus. Students following GNVQ (General National Vocational Qualification) courses were selected as the focus group and the numbers of times they used the library, the lengths of each time etc. were noted. Additonally, some students were interviewed as to how helpful they found the library and also a brief questionnaire was completed. Although Tina had always seen these students as some of the keenest, she did not expect to learn so much from them.

> *They* asked the questions, once they knew what was going on, *they* advised me as to how the library could service them even better; *they* suggested how it might help students on other courses. They also knew all staff attitudes to the library – not that I asked them! I shall continue to use questionnaires as a regular part of monitoring the quality of service the library provides, but some of the questions will be far more searching now for the older students.

The relationship between the GNVQ students and the librarian altered to that of a partnership of learners, in Tina's view. This, she feels, has enabled her to relate her services more closely to the needs of the student learners.

Mel (Northamptonshire school) investigated homework at her school, which included questioning students about the way their homework was marked.

> It was a revelation. The students were so perceptive. We, the staff, put a grade and then, in line with good professional practice, we put comments as all best practice tells us that's monitoring and feedback. The students were, independently, quite clear that if you have a grade, you don't read the comments. What's the point? Comments are much better than grades but they'll only read them when there isn't a grade! As well as being a shock to my system, it told me something – we never talk to kids about that kind of thing, like how *we* mark *your* work. We explain grades in booklets but we don't discuss.

Mel's discovery and her further discussions with students subsequently developed strongly her own notion of an effective learning relationship between teacher and student.

Similarly, Carole (same school) in researching the appropriateness of the ethos in Year 7 (intake year for an 11–18 school) found the 11-year-olds remarkably insightful as far as their new school's offerings were concerned, but also acknowledged she and others had underestimated what these students could offer *if asked*.

> We were a kind, caring school, keen to be nice to them, but they wanted more.

The relationship, Carole realised, needed to be more reciprocal.

An assignment on a similar topic in a Leicester school revealed a need for a readjustment of relationships following students' views being gathered looking back upon the highly structured induction programme they had received in the first week of their arrival in the new secondary school. With the wisdom of one term behind them, the 11-year-olds asked why they had not been told about the courses, curriculum etc. They had of course been given this in great detail in the first week.

> In effect, we discovered that we had bombarded them with good stuff from our point of view when all they'd wanted to know was where the toilets were and how they could make sure they didn't lose their bags and coats. When I suggested to them that this was the outcome of my research, one of them said scornfully 'Well, we could have told you that if you'd asked us then!' Perhaps my research is redundant now, but I wouldn't have found out otherwise.
>
> (Gwen, Leicester school)

(iii) Teachers as students. It is standard practice for many tutors to comment to serving teachers on courses or projects that they are students again and certainly I have regularly used the comment lightheartedly to reassure teachers re-commencing study after a long period. One of the questions put to teacher researchers asking whether being a student had had any effect upon their own practice and behaviour elicited powerful responses. Sixty per cent of teachers were 'very confident' that their own relationships with students that they taught had been influenced for the better, both in the actual classroom teaching and in their general involvement with students, e.g. as form tutor, head of year or house or department. One teacher even commented that when she was on duty at breaktime and saw students doing homework due in the following lesson, she now went and helped them.

> Previously, I'd have told them off and lectured them for not doing it the night before!
>
> (Pauline, Kettering school)

The model of reflective practitioner involved in a teacher's typical research assignment will have the following elements (Terrell *at al.*, 1998, p. 16):

Defining a tight and appropriate focus;
Reading literature;
Thinking;
Collecting first hand data;
Asking questions;
The process of writing;
Analysing and evaluating evidence.

The skills involved in this, although to a different standard, will be similar to those demanded by some coursework at GCSE and at post-16 level. This alone enabled some teachers to see parallels and share with students in those contexts some of their own experiences. Liz (Bedfordshire school) said that she explained to her students how she had to carry out a similar task to the one she was asking of them and the whole process became a shared one not simply something the students had to do 'for the teacher'.

However, the main effect upon the relationship between teacher as student and the school students came through the empathy discovered in sharing the actual experience of being students at the same time as each other. There were extremes in the descriptions of the effects upon attitude of teacher towards student, from 'I'm much tougher on them now, as I have to do it, so do they' (Sue, Bedfordshire School), to 'I'm much more sympathetic now' (Zoe, same school). The majority of teachers, some unconsciously and some deliberately, had increased understanding of the demands of learning which were placed upon young people at school. Some felt it was a strong affirmation of a 'firm but fair' approach they had always tried to adopt, reinforced by their being in the same situation. As Julian (Corby school) put it:

> It made me glad I'd been sympathetic to *my* students but that I had imposed deadlines.

A number of teachers openly shared their current research and writing experiences with students to increase motivation on both sides. Carole (Northamptonshire school) at one point, in encouraging GCSE students to complete coursework projects, had shown her group her own half-written research assignment report.

> I said, 'Look, I've got to get this finished and handed in by the end of the month, and I've got a thousand other things to do as well, just like you. If I can do it, so can you!

Wendy (same school) recalled that 'The sixth form tease me. "Have you got your work in yet, Miss?"'

She noted that on her first research assignment she had made some of the same mistakes the students made, i.e. not balanced her work out carefully in time and not focused her investigation sufficiently.

> The very mistakes I had told them off for! I hadn't understood properly before that they have to juggle the demands of three Advanced Levels at the same time and their work in my subject is one part of that. Of course, I knew *as a fact* that mine was one of three they were doing but I understand what it means now I have to juggle this piece of research and the reading into all my other teaching and preparation and marking.

Judy (Bedfordshire school) used the same principle as exhortation in the summer term of 1998.

> Look, I've got this to do and all these other things and mark your work. *And* I'm going to watch the World Cup on television just like you! We can all do it.

Jo Fl (Corby school) felt she could relate more to the sheer frustration of students.

> Now when they say 'I can't do this, Miss,' instead of feeling so exasperated, I think 'I feel like that sometimes.' And that's it. It's knowing how they *feel*, even if logically you know as the person who showed them they must *be able* to do it.

Jackie (programme co-ordinator at Northants school) and Tim (head of same school) had both seen this increased empathy for student learning in the teacher researchers. Jackie felt it was important for students to see their teachers as learners. Tim agreed, but said it was difficult to assess the spread of this particular attitude across other staff, although he was sure it was happening in the teams directly affected by the teachers concerned.

> Of course, I think all these teachers were empathetic learners in the first place, perhaps some had lost the habit a little. I've got to believe all good teachers have it.

Jane (same school) described how she transferred to herself precisely the motivational tactics she had employed for years with students:

> Right down to rewarding myself with a bar of chocolate – when I felt it was deserved for how much I'd done at that point.

Although most of the direct transfer, at least in openly expressed form, related to students of 14 years and above, there were some references to younger students. Jo Fe (Corby school) referred to the fact that she tried to get her 12- and 13-year-olds now to organise their own timetables for themselves more and to help each other more. 'You rely on other people with *your* studies, so I realise they have to as well.'

In attempting to summarise the positive effects of in-house teacher research upon teacher-student relationship, it seems reasonable to bring together the importance of the teacher as role model and a widely accepted aspect of effective student learning, that of high expectations (e.g. Creemers, 1994). The evidence given above suggests that students can be impressed by teachers as learners, or at least that those teachers firmly believe it is motivating for students to know of this. In sharing mutual learning experiences, including those concerned with the 'quality of instruction' (*ibid.*), such as time planning, reviewing work, evaluation etc, there are grounds for optimism that teachers' effectiveness may increase, in addition to the application of specific outcomes of their research. For students passing a classroom an hour after the end of normal schooling and watching curiously a group of their teachers 'in class', it was natural for those students to ask the next day: 'How are you getting on with your learning? It's a fair question' (Middlewood and Parker, 1998, p. 56).

(b) Relationships between Staff

In general terms, the effect upon staff relationships with other staff is best described by the increased emphasis upon collaborative learning. The process of involving other colleagues in their own investigations and of sharing process and outcomes with fellow researchers was described by a majority of teachers (60 per cent of respondents) as having a 'powerful' positive influence upon the overall ethos of the staffroom and school in general. Case studies of this cultural impact are described in Chapter 3; a few of the relationships with special factors are now examined.

STAFF IN SCHOOLS IN DIFFICULTIES

During the period under discussion, two of the schools involved were in extremely difficult circumstances. School A was due for closure by the LEA within two years of the course linked to research assignments being set up. Undoubtedly, the then headteacher and senior staff saw the main aim to enable existing teachers to gain what accreditation they could, enhancing their prospects for job-seeking. The maintaining of motivation was also a second stated aim. School B was in Special Measures when the school-based research course was established. During that actual period, an LEA Review brought the news that the school was to be closed. The situations in these two schools offered evidence that, since the direct aim for school improvement could hardly be deemed to be relevant as the schools would no longer exist, the benefits must lie in the process, firstly for maintaining and enhancing the motivation of teachers in potentially very demotivating circumstances and, secondly, enabling the school's students to receive the best possible service during the schools' remaining time.

As Allan (programme manager School B) put it:

> Respect, no; admiration for my colleagues is what I feel. Their first concern was for the students still in the school. 'Anything we can find out to make our teaching better for them now has got to be good', they said. And of course if they get an extra qualification and perhaps a job, that's a bonus.

Allan felt that the extra confidence given to teachers by their own research and the debate it generated was considerable. Phil (same school) felt he learned more about the professionalism and intellectual ability of colleagues in the period of the research than in years previously of working with them. David (School B) said that his research made him look at his own practice, but also to reflect on how changes were normally initiated.

> I realised that, like many schools, we had written good policies and, sometimes, checked on whether they were being implemented. What we hadn't done was find out whether any of our new changes were having an impact.

As Lynda (School B) said:

> The research enabled me much more to find out people's feelings about the job. Not in the general staffroom way, but specifically why someone did or did not, for example, like doing this or that in the classroom.

In School B, about half of the teaching staff were involved in the research-based course, and some of the above quotations illustrate that the group research had a strong influence upon staff morale and unity at a time when it was needed. In School A, the proportion of staff was even greater. Seventeen of the 21 staff committed themselves initially to the programme (everyone except those opting for retirement when the school closed). Numbers reduced, of course, as staff gained posts elsewhere, some of them promoted, and one practical difficulty was evident. With so many staff involved in data collection and the number of students small and decreasing, the scope for student involvement had to be limited. The emphasis in research was placed therefore on staff, management, resources etc, and on the relevant external components such as parents and community. The commitments and enthusiasm of the research group were seen as powerful. Alison (School A) described how the discussion about data collected, about processes, and about helping each other:

> took over breaktimes, lunchtimes and many meetings. It stopped us dwelling on the misery of our situation and we'd become animated. That was important for two reasons. It reminded us we were professionals, with professional pride, who should be discussing management, teaching, learning, the curriculum and so on. Also, it meant we went into the next lesson animated for the students and they deserved and needed that in the school, which was dying on its feet in the last year.

Diane (School A) was in the unenviable position of having moved from a school that had closed four years earlier. For her the course and the research had been a 'salvation'.

> I know none of it was my fault, and knew I could find out about improving my practice and school. I wanted to show myself and any future employer that I was committed to improvement, which I am. What kept me going was sharing what I'd found with the others. We were all incredibly helpful to each other.

Jenny (School A) found research an:

> amazing eye-opener. I found out so much about myself, as well as others. When you ask structured questions – of parents, students, or staff – and they're taken seriously, you start to ask then of yourself and you question certain assumptions you've had. Of course, plenty that you've been doing is fine but things don't stand still. When you've been teaching a number of years, you have general views about children, parents and so on, but until you get the data properly together, you don't realise some of those views are based upon the past.

PART-TIME STAFF

A few of the teachers involved were on part-time contracts when they began the research work, all of them female. Sue (Corby school) confessed that the work had affected her relationships at school in two ways.

> It's so easy to feel left out when you're part-time. Belonging to the group – and the 'catch-up' group – well, we were all the same, because we were doing the same. In fact, as I didn't work on Fridays, I was able to come in then and interview some Heads of Departments – which others envied. Otherwise, doing research was hell for the family. When you're part-time, all family arrangements, such as child care, are carefully worked out. Still, in the group, I was exactly the same as all the rest.

Also, Sue's own research into the role of the middle manager:

> opened my eyes, because I'd not previously structured my ideas – and I do
> intend to be one. I've become ultra-critical of some middle managers; yet I
> understand more and I think they should!

When Sue did her second piece of research, she found herself using a conceptual framework developed through the first and examining colleagues' approaches to work according to this framework:

> For example, thinking what might be the real motivation behind actions – not
> sinister, just real when perhaps they didn't even know it themselves.

Fiona's (Northamptonshire school) confidence in her own ability grew 'enormously' through the research. Again, as a part-timer:

> and I think it's women too. Virtually all the part-timers are women and we
> lack a bit of confidence and we don't have that competitiveness.

By researching into management styles within her own school, Fiona felt she questioned her own style as well as others'.

> I don't just accept now. I analyse more and doing research just makes you clear
> that you know more of what's really going on. I can say 'actually, that isn't
> true', when you hear a generalised statement and it's not just your prejudiced
> opinion given back. At the very least, you can say 'I'm not sure I agree'. I
> wonder how many times this does actually happen. Maybe we could find out.

Jo Fe (Corby school), a part-time teacher, actually did an investigation into the management of part-time staff across a number of schools, coming to the conclusion that her own school was as good as any and better than many!

> This was very reassuring. It gave me more confidence and more faith in my
> own managers.

ASSOCIATE STAFF

Relationships between teaching and non-teaching (associate) staff were affected in some of the schools involved. These were in three ways: (1) by the outcomes of the actual research e.g. appraisal or induction of associate staff; (2) by associate staff being sources of data for teachers in their research and in a small number of cases (3) by actually doing research themselves. The fact that relationships changed because of (1) was not just that new programmes were introduced but that they were introduced as a result of research, which examined good practice, and for example, identified needs through questioning the relevant personnel. Linda

(Warwickshire school) investigated the management of Learning Support Assistants in her school but discovered an aspect of the assistants' perceptions which had significance. Her school (recently awarded Investors in People (IIP) status) had a formal approach to recognition and training of these associate staff. However, Linda's research found they felt they were not 'valued at all' by teaching colleagues, especially senior staff, despite formal recognition. Cultural indicators, such as limited access to staffroom and not being included on 'staff lists' that were circulated, led the Assistants to believe that they did not matter and that their opinions were not sought. An important aspect of the sensitive management of people was highlighted by the teacher's research.

Perhaps the most powerful impact upon relationships came when Associate Staff themselves undertook research. At a Special school in Oxford, John joined the teachers on the research group 'for experience and for the school'. Two of the research assignments he carried out were influential in school operations. One, involving the behaviour of the students outside of class, had the effect of making the school re-examine its practice in this area and was described by Mark (Programme Manager) as 'one of the most important pieces of work done here'. That, and the interchange of ideas and processes involved in the group developed the relationships. John was on equal terms as a researcher, earning powerful respect from colleagues and John himself was ready to admit that:

> although I worked with teachers and liked them, I tended to think that as a group they weren't in touch with the real world. Through the course and the projects, I've found out the reality. My views on teachers and education have changed a lot.

Mark said that although relationships between teachers and support staff were always strong in a special school ('they have to be'), the involvement of both in joint research work, not just doing a course together, had been a 'strong professional bonding'. Perhaps an example such as this is the most powerful, involving as it does someone like John, a mature person with no formal academic qualifications, epitomising the importance of the collaborative nature of *all* those who work in the school in their commitment to improvement for the students. Mark's view was that John's status, involving a slightly different relationship with students from teachers had, possibly, enabled him to 'tap' aspects of their responses not available to teachers, especially in the area of behaviour.

Clearly, in the other schools, there were qualified graduate associate staff who did research and it is possible that the above point may have been relevant to, for example, the two librarians (one in a secondary school, one in a Further Education college) who undertook investigations with students.

RELATIONSHIPS BETWEEN SENIOR MANAGERS AND STAFF

In four of the schools involved, the headteachers joined research groups themselves, two for one module only, two for the whole of the time. One of the latter two joined all the discussions and preparations but did not actually carry out research himself.

> I felt as soon as I would be asking the questions, staff would question why I wanted to know – even though I joined in all the discussions and encouraged sharing the results and helped to implement some of what was found.

Two of the other headteachers continued their research in other external contexts and the fourth retired before the group had completed. These heads in general were unsure about their involvement.

> I feel I'm inhibiting, although I try not to be ... if the research is as challenging as it should be, I've got to be challenged. I can't afford to be seen putting any brakes on what might be looked at.

Hopkins *et al.* (1994, p. 152) remind us that methods for in-school inquiry should be chosen which 'will be acceptable to those who are likely to be involved', but this acceptability should not be determined by the leadership of the organisation because of a perceived worry about a threat to the status quo:

> Bureaucratic means may satisfy the organisational 'top' of the institution, but this does not necessarily bring about desired effects!
>
> (Bollen, 1996, p. 7)

These heads appeared to realise that the desired effects (of positive change) would come from below the top and that the 'top' should not appear to be attempting to steer the means.

Altogether, the involvement of headteachers in carrying out research therefore is not especially successful. In most schools, impact upon relationships between teachers and senior managers came about through the interactions involved in carrying out the actual research and the dissemination and sharing of the results of the research. In research into management in schools, senior managers inevitably become the sources of data collection and are often targeted for semi-structured interview. Barbara (Deputy Principal, Bedfordshire school) felt that, in addition to being able to relate to some colleagues more through the professional discussions engendered, some of the research assignments and what she gleaned from the discussions showed that staff knew less about policy planning than had been assumed: 'It shows we need to look hard at our management/staff communications.'

Similarly, Den (Leicester school) said that the research had brought home the importance of communication at all levels:

> not assuming that people know because they have been told. You have to ensure that everyone who has a stake in an initiative realises what it will mean for them.

Several teachers reported that the experience of approaching, interviewing and sharing results with line managers had given them confidence in themselves and their relationships with their managers. It was equally encouraging to find senior managers believing that they had seen some staff in a new light through the probing of some research. Richard (Head, Corby school) reported that he had learned so much more about some teachers and also seen their confidence grow that he had no hesitation in asking them to take on particular appropriate tasks now, because he knew 'they will do the ground work necessary before just plunging in.'

Howard (Programme Manager, Wellingborough school) described how in his school several members of the Senior Management Team took responsibility for working with individual researchers 'in a kind of mentoring role', and this enabled each teacher to have a different relationship with individual senior staff.

CONCLUSION

The effects of having a significant number of staff within a school involved in carrying out small-scale research projects can have effects that are wider than the cumulative effect of the results and applications of those projects. The effects upon the individuals as reflective professionals can be considerable, especially when they are involved in regular group work, which appears to facilitate collaborative practice. Furthermore, the existence of such a group and its activities can have a significant effect upon the relationships within the school, not only involving group members, but on other groupings (e.g. senior managers, associate staff) and, not least, upon the central relationship of teacher and student.

In the following chapter, three schools are examined in which in-house research may well have had a considerable impact on whole school culture. However, we do not possess evidence which suggests that the effect upon relationships in a school will necessarily permeate the whole school. The exceptional circumstances of the two closing schools described in this chapter meant that (a) the schools had relatively small numbers of staff and (b) there was a 'unity of purpose' among staff brought about by their position.

Of the 72 teachers who responded in the survey, only four said that they were 'doubtful' whether their research affected the whole school in any way, but 18 were 'unsure'. What is significant perhaps is that all these 22 were teachers who were one of a small group of teachers/researchers (two to four) in their schools. The 50 teachers/researchers who were 'very confident' (27) or 'confident' (23) of affecting the whole school all came from groups which constituted a higher proportion of the total staffing of the school. Other factors, such as the relative separateness of different faculties, for example, or channels of communication were not explored in this survey. It is possible that the culture of the organisation may be the over-riding consideration, and the following chapter examines some of this possibility.

7

INFLUENCING SCHOOL CULTURE

David Middlewood

INTRODUCTION

This chapter examines the extent to which research in schools carried out by its staff has influenced the ethos or culture of that school. Given that impact may be greater the more pieces of research are carried out, the chapter focuses on schools where a significant number of staff have been involved, using the concept of the ideal school culture as being that of the 'learning organisation'. Characteristics of this culture are proposed. The study uses three particular secondary schools, each at a slightly different stage of using numbers of staff to carry out research, and investigates the extent to which the characteristics are evident.

The study concludes that widespread practitioners' in-house research can be a very powerful tool for influencing the development of the school culture to that of a learning organisation. There is an attempt to identify the factors which appear to be important in managing this development, the most significant of which may be the willingness and support of school leaders and senior managers to encourage such research in the first place.

SCHOOL CULTURES AND THE LEARNING ORGANISATION

(a) Importance of Culture

Because schools have effective learning as central to their purpose, it is reasonable to propose that 'the school as a learning organisation' might be the aim for leaders in their quest for the most appropriate school culture. If culture is most simply defined as 'the way we do things round here' (Deal, 1985), it can be seen as trying to capture the informal, implicit – often unconscious – side of an organisation. Culture may take its expression in patterns of thought and behaviour which give meaning to the place of work.

> Meaning derives from elements of culture: shared values and beliefs, heroes and heroines, stories and an informal network of cultural players.
>
> (Deal, 1985, p. 607)

I shall argue that, in the schools examined, the staff carrying out research become these 'cultural players' through developing their own informal network.

The assumption behind the notion of school culture as being important in change is that interaction between members of the organisation, or its sub-groups, eventually leads to behavioural norms that gradually become cultural features of the school.

> The nature of a culture is found in its social norms and customs.
>
> (Morgan, 1986, p. 12)

Underpinning belief in the importance of culture is the assumption that:

> beliefs, values and ideology are at the heart of organisations. Individuals hold certain ideas and value-preferences which influence how they behave and how they view the behaviour of other members.
>
> (Bush, 1995, p. 130)

(b) The Learning Organisation

As Bush (1998, p. 32) suggests that interest in culture 'may be explained, in part, as dissatisfaction with the limitations of the traditional, bureaucratic model', so Lumby (1997) summarises the interest in the application of the learning organisation concept to education as being in, part, a realisation that conventional training of individual teachers could not prepare schools for managing change on a new unprecedented scale.

This emphasis on 'a more holistic and communal approach' (Lumby, 1997, p. 32) is relevant to our investigations into whether significant numbers of teachers operating in a particular way (i.e. by carrying out and writing up research) influence the development of the school towards becoming a 'learning school'. By selecting research as the means of developing and encouraging the capacity to learn, it can be argued that school leaders were achieving the central strategic task that Lumby (1997) suggests faces them. 'Staff development' in this concept is not something that can be viewed discretely, even though the budget heading for a particular innovation to stimulate it may be thus titled. Senge's (1991) point that 'learning' had lost all but a general meaning for many people and that 'taking in information is only distantly related to real learning' (*ibid.*, p. 13) was powerfully understood by leaders in the three schools studied who were all clear that, among other reasons for commencing a programme based on in-school research, one important one was the 'need for teachers to learn by doing is as crucial as what they find out' (Kate, Assistant Principal, Samuel Whitbread College). Richard, Head of Lodge Park School, was clear that the hope was 'to create a learning buzz' and Tim, Head of Campion School, was unequivocal: 'Good teachers are good learners and *what* they learn may be secondary; they must *want* to learn.'

(c) Characteristics of Learning Organisation

Aspinwall and Pedlar (1997) suggest that, in trying to understand the totality of learning in an organisation, it is helpful to think of learning as of different types:

1. Learning *about* things

2. Learning to *do* things

3. Learning to *become ourselves, to achieve full potential*

4. Learning to *achieve things together.*

(Adapted from Aspinwall and Pedlar, 1997, p. 230)

They suggest that the pressures of mandatory changes in education in recent years have emphasised the first two at the expense of the second two. As one of the heads in this study noted: 'We are probably a successful school by many people's standards, but it's not enough. We can stop thinking and that "we" includes me.'

Clearly, when teachers engage in research in their own schools, one of the purposes of each piece of research is to gain knowledge (Type 1). Equally, the researcher gains in skills (Type 2) in the research process itself. Especially when doing more than one investigation, the teacher refines and develops those skills e.g. in developing methodologies, ascertaining the appropriateness of particular methodologies, and in focused reading.

However, it is probably Types 3 and 4 that will have the most impact upon any development of a school's learning culture. As people discover things about themselves ('to become ourselves'), values and attitudes are formed and gradually become behavioural norms. When a group of staff is involved, the opportunity for learning 'to achieve things together' is increased.

Aspinwall and Pedlar (1997, p. 240) identify what they see as key characteristics of a 'learning school' which include:

- A commitment to lifelong learning for all those within the school.
- An emphasis on collaborative learning and the creative and positive use of difference and conflict.
- A holistic understanding of the school as an organisation.

Such characteristics are not easily measurable of course and 'commitment', 'emphasis' and 'understanding' are terms which relate to a cultural concept such as the 'learning organisation,' rather than any set of visible criteria. Indeed, staff within a school with such a culture may never use the term 'learning organisation' or discuss it, they simply have a deeper sense of awareness of learning.

THE SCHOOLS IN THE STUDY

School A

Lodge Park School is an 11–18 comprehensive school in the Northamptonshire town of Corby. Formerly a 'British Steel town', Corby has had to develop alternative industries in the 1980s and 1990s. Lodge Park is situated on the northern edge of the town facing a large local authority housing estate and, at the rear, across an 'A' road the open lands of a stately home estate. The school's intake comes primarily from the housing estate and the vast majority of the students live within walking distance. The numbers on roll have expanded in the 1990s to approximately 1,000. The school became Grant Maintained in 1992 and it gained Technology College status in 1994. Richard (Parker) became Headteacher in 1993 and the school has gained significant amounts of sponsorship, enabling new buildings such as a new technology block, a Millennium Centre and greatly enlarged sports centre to be built. Examination results have improved steadily and since 1997 the school has been over-subscribed for places. It has thus made great progress in the 1990s and is part of one of the proposed 'Action Zones' in 2000.

When the Masters programme commenced in the Autumn of 1994, to be taught fully in the school and from which the individual research projects would originate, the Head had been in post one year. An indicator of the way staff were loyal to the school was that the Head had found that the five other members of his Senior Management Team had a total of 137 years service in Lodge Park School! The Autumn 1994 group had 13 members, 11 of whom completed research assignments. Ten of these continued to the next module of the programme and they were joined by one new teacher and four others already on the staff of the school, including one of the Deputy Heads (28 years service in the school) and the Head of Business Studies, who was later to become the Programme Co-ordinator. At the time of writing, all these 15 staff are still at the school, although others have of course joined the school and the group and some moved on to another school during that time. Well over 80 individual research assignments have been carried out by staff, mostly at the level of those requiring work to be written up in about 5,000 words but more than a dozen recently or currently involving larger scale Masters dissertation research (20,000 words).

Lodge Park School therefore is a school where in-house practitioner research has occurred on a large scale, over about four years. Furthermore, most of the staff involved (which included two part-time teachers and the graduate school librarian), were already at the school prior to this initiative and have remained there; a significant number expect to continue there.

School B

Campion School is a rural 11–18 comprehensive school situated on the edge of the village of Bugbrooke, also in Northamptonshire. Its number on roll is nearly 1,200 and its intake is mixed, although socio-economically quite 'favoured'. Seventy per cent of students arrive at school by bus.

The school was achieving pass rates at GCSE (A-C) which were around the national average, but in 1996–97, through a series of initiatives, raised its rate from 46 per cent to 61 per cent. Campion School might conveniently be described as having been in danger of becoming a 'cruising school' but the 1997 performance established its capabilities as a high performing one. Tim (Bartlett) had become Headteacher in 1989 and, at the time of writing, was due to leave for a further headship elsewhere.

The school had a significant proportion of its staff, especially in Senior Teacher and middle management positions, who had worked there for more than 12 years. It had also a turn-over among younger staff who were appointed and left after a few years for promotion to middle management positions.

The school-based programme at Campion began in 1995 with a group of seven staff and has proceeded through four modules (by the end of 1998). Unlike Lodge Park, a number of different people joined for one module only, some to leave the school, others not. A constant group of six teachers (seven, but one gained promotion and left) remained who had carried out all the research assignments. These were a mix of those new to the school, those long-serving, and included one part-time teacher.

Campion School therefore had a smaller number of staff involved in research, but had, like Lodge Park, a constant group. The individuals had not done as many research assignments as those in School A and none of the dissertation research scale. However, the group contained a mix of long-serving and relatively new staff and the circumstances of the school in its intake, performance and the fact that the Head had been in post for eight years when the initiative began made it likely to be quite different in culture from School A.

School C

The Samuel Whitbread Community College is a 13–18 maintained establishment in Bedfordshire LEA. The College was founded in 1973. Numbers of students on roll in the 1990s have increased considerably to the point where the College is currently oversubscribed. There are 1,120 currently on roll. The intake is largely urban/rural, with a genuine comprehensive mix. Examination results are above County and National averages.

The College is proud of its place in the community and is a large centre for adult education. There is also a nursery on site.

The College is a centre for excellence for Initial Teacher Training, leading a local consortium, and is recognised as an Investor in People.

The school-based programme was established in February 1998 and 11 of the 12 teachers carried out their first research assignments. Ten staff plan to continue (two have left for promotion elsewhere). The school therefore is at an early stage of school-based research development but already had experience of a number of teachers active in this. All the staff involved were full-time, but one teacher was on maternity leave at the time of the first module and attended – with the baby!

All three schools had one person in an influential position who helped to initiate the programme. Richard, Head of Lodge Park, Jackie, Professional Development Tutor at Campion, and Kate, Assistant Principal at Samuel Whitbread, had each had *recent* experience, as Masters students, of carrying out research in their own schools. They were each convinced of the value for their schools and individual staff.

METHODOLOGY

At Schools A and B, as each person commenced a second and subsequent piece of research, they were interviewed about their learning from previous work and about the perceived impact or specific follow-up on the research in school, or on the individual. Semi-structured interviews were later held with 11 of the 15 School A core group who had reached the stage described earlier. Six of the seven at School B were similarly interviewed. At Samuel Whitbread, a group discussion was held with nine of the group, followed by individual interviews with eight members of the group. Additionally, semi-structured interviews were held with two or three senior managers in each school (Head, Programme Co-ordinator and Budget Manager in School A; Head and Training Co-ordinator in School B; Assistant Principal and Deputy Principal in School C). The schools' own documentation involving evaluation of the programmes and the relevance of the research project was also made available.

THE FINDINGS

(1) Learning about Oneself/Self-Development

Every single person interviewed referred to a growth in self-esteem achieved through the discovery process involved in the research. The aspects of this seemed clear. First, staff had found out *for themselves* the actuality or truth in certain situations and felt able to give opinions and present views and recommendations with a confidence that arises from authoritative, first-hand knowledge. Secondly, the actual process of doing research involving questioning people, approaching some not normally associated with, brought a confidence in the individual's ability to carry out the process. Thirdly, the reading, to provide the context within which their own research fitted, gave individuals increased awareness of conceptual frameworks within which they could place practice which they considered routine. As Fiona (School B) said: 'I had been content to go along in my own furrow, doing a good, conscientious job. The insight I have gained into what's really going on in my own school, under my nose, is surprising.'

Chris (Deputy Head in School A), with 28 years in the school in various posts, described how she had felt capable within her own area of knowledge. This (School A) was the professional world she knew and did not see why major changes might be needed. The arrival of a new headteacher in 1993, she now says, worried her as it was obvious changes would occur. Although she supported the principle of the school-based Masters beginning in 1994, she did not join the original group herself, partly because, as she now confesses, she did not believe she could do it. With Jo Fl., and Sue (a part-time teacher), both also with considerable reservations, she joined the second module. The three of them formed an additional mini-support group, helping each other so successfully that they have 'caught up' with the original group.

> The whole process has been an enormous lift for my personal self-esteem. When I collected all the data in from my first piece of research (on appraisal of clerical and administrative staff), I looked at it and thought 'That's mine. I did that. No one else has done that!' Although I wasn't too sure at that stage how to use it, I realised that I'd done something I had never done before in all those years. The more I looked at what I'd got, the more I realised it was real, not just what I'd assumed or thought it might be. From then on, my brain has never stopped buzzing about possibilities for research.
>
> (Chris, School A)

Chris W. (School A), saying that the process had given 'a lot more confidence', mentioned that the requirement to write up the research had frightened her initially. 'I had not written an essay for 20 years'. Not being able to type, she had found it slow work but among her future plans now were precise targets for her own word-processing.

Several teachers mentioned the increased confidence to raise issues at staff or departmental meetings.

> Because I know I've done the spade-work, or read about other research or know of research other group members have done, I feel that I won't be put down as not important, even though I haven't been here as many years as the others. Previously, I thought they'd just think 'Well, she's only young. What does she know?
>
> (Mel, School B)

Wendy (School B) mentioned how the increased confidence helped in her situation in being new to the school when the programme began: 'because you can understandably be dismissed somewhat early on as you don't know the situation here'.

Several others mentioned the greater confidence in approaching their line managers to make a point. Some of this came from the knowledge that their views were data-based but some also from the sheer experience of the interaction with people, often senior, not often encountered except in day-to-day matters.

> Interviewing the Head on the basis of a professional dialogue was quite new and changed my perceptions of him and his role. I would not have dreamed of going and simply discussing an educational issue with him once. Now, I seek his advice regularly and both our opinions count.
>
> (Jo Fe, School A)

Shelagh (School C) felt that the research and the reading, in widening her own horizons after just one research assignment, now enabled her to discuss current issues confidently within a conceptual framework with student teachers in school on teaching practice. 'Previously, it was sometimes embarrassing that some of them knew more than we experienced teachers did. Now, I can hold my own!' It was Shelagh who described that having to make recommendations following research findings was 'frightening'.

Jane (School C):

> Yes, because you know that they will have to be carried out. But carrying out the research makes you know you're dealing with how it really is. It makes you feel good about yourself.

For Tina, the School Librarian (School A), the confidence gained in doing her own investigations related to the ability to share process and findings with teaching colleagues.

> As a returner to the profession, I wanted somehow to relate my work to the needs of the school. Carrying out the research and involving teaching colleagues in the process has helped change perceptions of the role of the librarian in the curriculum. Librarians don't just stamp books!

Further evidence of growth in self-confidence was in the teachers' ability to choose their own topics for research. Tim (Head of School B) commented:

> Initially people always used to be coming to me to ask what they should do. Now, I haven't seen anyone for that reason for over a year. They're on a roll; they've got their own momentum now.

(2) Learning to Achieve Things Together

Every single person said that they had found the support of the school group and the opportunity to work with others one of the most valuable and important factors in the success of the research programmes. Fifteen of the 25 teachers interviewed were adamant that they could not have continued the programme without the school peer group support.

Part of this, for some teachers, as exemplified by Jo Fl. (School A), was a shared understanding of the pressures and problems faced by group members. As Jo explained:

> I knew that others, especially women, had the same problems of time, family, shopping that I had and it helped in two ways. One, we talked about them together, which helped, and the other was the thought that if she can cope and still find time to read and research, so can I!

Mutual support became part of the process in the groups ranging from the practical (Julian in School A became the group's unofficial 'helper', giving lifts to a colleague without transport and offering to spiral-bind all written assignments of group members), to the instinctive. When one teacher in School A was sick and away from school, two other colleagues distributed and collected her questionnaires for her – and 'nagged' some late respondents on her behalf!

In addition to the 'catch-up' sub-group described earlier, other sub-groups formed. Mel (School B) described how three teachers supported each other by utilising different research strengths.

> If I'm stuck, I'll ring up Claire and ask if she's any ideas about what I do next. I always used to ask you (i.e. the tutor). She's never short of an idea and even if I don't use her particular idea it gets me going again. Also, Carole is good on the reading – that's her real strength; whereas I'm good at statistical analysis. I love compiling data and doing the analysis.

This was independently confirmed by Carole who said she often turned to Mel to help her make initial sense of data she'd found. In no way however did the existence of these sub-groups balkanise the whole group ethos. Carole was adamant that every member of School B's group had and gave support. 'We inspired each other.'

School C's comments on the importance of group support and collaboration reflected that of the other schools in the earliest stages. 'Reassurance' (Charles) often came in the form of jokes and competition – feigned or real: 'You swot!' 'How many words have you done then?'

These elements of reassurance in collaboration, with an initial hint of competition, were well illustrated by Richard's (Head of School A) recollection of the moment when assessments of the group's first research assignments were returned to the school. In line with the University's procedure, assignments were graded and obviously it is the first one which is most anxiously awaited.

> For some reason, Chris W. was not in the staffroom and at mid-morning break teachers were exchanging news of their assessment with each other and with staff generally. Someone had peeped at Chris's grade and had seen she'd got an A, the only person that first time. When she came into the staffroom at coffee time, spontaneous applause broke out – coming not just from others on the course but from all staff. It was a wonderful moment and the most memorable of my headship, which I shall never forget. It will only be surpassed when they all graduate with their Masters!

A powerful feature of the school research groups was that they had no other obvious coherence. Both Kate and Judy described the group at School C as 'an odd combination of people', in the sense that they were people who had nothing obviously in common as a group, came from different parts of the schools and consequently brought together some people who had never had occasion to work together previously. This was now seen as one of its strengths. As Judy discovered in her own research into the school's concept of the effectiveness of a head of department:

There is little sharing of good practice across departments – we don't talk about it. Perhaps we're defensive about our departmental practice.

Even those teachers who described themselves as independent learners, such as Julian (School A) and Linda (School C), were quick to recognise the importance of the collaborative aspect of learning. Julian found the camaraderie of the group 'amazingly motivating'. Linda described herself as someone who, as a student, had 'gone my own way' and therefore, like Julian and Lyn (School C), assumed further research would be the same. 'Now I know that my students need the support from their peers, just as I did doing this work!'

The collaboration and support offered to each other by research group members often took the form of unplanned discussions, 'talking shops' and 'surgeries' upon the methodologies or specific issues involved in an individual's research. As Steve (School A) describes it:

> After a while, you could be confident you could mention a problem or share progress with someone else doing research. It would not just be of the 'how's it going?' type query. People were actually *empathetic* [my emphasis]. People were capable of discussing a specific problem they'd got with you; even though they didn't know the details, they knew what the questions were, suggested a new angle on the situation and so on.

One of the important issues in examining collaborative learning as part of a whole school progress towards being a learning organisation is inevitably the extent to which those *not* involved in doing the research as part of a group were involved. In all three schools, the group members made two points strongly: (1) people at all levels were generally very supportive and co-operative and (2) they were in the early stages very surprised at just how supportive these others were. Judy (School C) was 'amazed' at how willing Heads of Departments were to be interviewed and indeed had thanked her at the end for 'the opportunity to talk about their own practice'. They told her, she said, that it had been an invaluable opportunity to reflect. 'I never get or take the time to do it normally. You've made me think and put it into words', as one Head of Department described it to her. Judy reasonably believed this to be an indication of the pressures under which teachers currently work, losing the chance to step back from daily operational matters.

Despite the relatively random nature of the make-up of the research groups, inevitably in all three schools some teachers operated in the same area(s) of the school, thus enabling further collaboration to occur during normal working times. The presence of four members of the Technology Department of School A, including the Head of Department, enabled those researchers not only to share discussions but also to support each other's research in the Department and, probably most importantly, to support implementation of each others' findings and recommendations, ensuring a complementary approach. In School C, even after one module, two members from the Modern Languages Department both examined different aspects of the related theme of boys' under-achievement, throwing light on the issue from both whole-school and departmental perspective. Honey (1991) suggested that development towards the learning organisation is possible in certain circumstances by creating:

> a mini learning organisation in the parts you *can* influence. Small incremental changes, if sustained, have a habit of gaining momentum to the point where they become transformational.
>
> (Honey, 1991, p. 33)

However, in the three schools studied, the interaction between the actual 'learning groups' and others in the schools appeared to be so positive that the need for a mini learning organisation did not arise. Jackie (Co-ordinator at School B) noted that some colleagues were concerned, rightly, that the actual research was of high quality and therefore played their part in this. Occasionally, a criticism of the quality of, for example, a questionnaire would be brought to her attention (not to the actual questionnaire composer's for fear of hurting feelings!). Jackie interpreted this herself as a desire to support *good* research, not research at any price.

Indeed, anxieties about the impact upon their colleagues came from the researchers themselves, not from the actual colleagues. They expressed concern about overload of colleagues and even, after one module, several at School C expressed concern about the pressure upon the Deputy Principal because she had been a key figure in curriculum research assignments for several people. Barbara (Deputy Principal at School C) did not express the same concern, having found the series of interviews 'refreshing' and 'challenging'. She had also found them 'enlightening', enabling her to meet and see certain teachers in a totally different light from her previous experience. This of course reflects the exact parallel to Jo Fe's comment, quoted earlier, about seeing her headteacher in a different light.

CHARACTERISTICS OF THE LEARNING SCHOOL

(1) A Commitment to Lifelong Learning

What indications were there that in the schools, those involved in the research learning would remain committed? In both School A and School B of course the first evidence came from the fact that a core group of staff had persisted beyond their first assignment to all and most of the stages involved in completing a Masters Degree. Eight of the 15 at School A were looking forward to gaining a higher degree (two of whom did not have a first degree), were certain they wanted it as recognition of what they had achieved, and as a mark of pride, but were clear that it was *not* for career enhancement prospects. Would the incentive for research and study continue? Some of the others hoped that it would help their career prospects but the same question still applied.

Most of the group members in Schools A and B felt that it would be very hard to give up research, reading and study, others that it would not be possible to do so. 'I couldn't stop now, even if I wanted to' (Chris W, School A) was a typical comment. Some of the habits, especially that of reading for research context, had become so ingrained that several teachers outlined specific strategies to continue. Mike and Chris W planned to continue membership of the University library 'by some means', while Liz (Co-ordinator at School A) had already renewed her membership of the Institute of Management Services, whose library is conveniently located in Corby, even though her Masters work is now complete.

> 'I now read the *TES* (*Times Educational Supplement*) properly', reported several teachers and several reported how their reading habits had changed from skimming documents to focused reading. 'I know what I'm looking for' (Zoe, School C). Chris W (School A) had been 'amazed at how much research already existed. I had no idea. Now, whenever I'll have a question, I'll think "someone must have looked into this already" and want to find out what's been found.'

A further ingrained habit mentioned is that of examining the evidence. Lyn (School C) described it well: 'I now accept that there are equally valid views to those I hold. I was previously a "right or wrong" person. Now if a recommendation is put forward that I don't like, I would be prepared to say "Well, I don't agree with it but there's the evidence and I have to accept it." My own research showed me evidence for aspects I didn't want to accept initially, but I'm a mathematician and the data was clear. I can remain more detached about proposals etc now and ensure and insist on genuine evidence being available as a basis for action.'

Liz (School A) became Programme Co-ordinator during and because of her involvement in the research programme. Her commitment to learning in the future is currently exemplified by her co-ordinating a new programme based at Lodge Park but involving teachers from mostly neighbouring primary schools as well as new Lodge Park staff.

(2) A Holistic Understanding of the School as an Organisation

Every single teacher bar one in the three schools said that the course and related research had widened their understanding of the school as a whole.

> People understand where they fit into the whole picture.
>
> (Steve, School A)

> People feel they are contributing to the whole school's development, whereas previously they knew what they did in their own area but didn't know how that linked with anything else, only how it compared.
>
> (Liz, School A)

Teachers understood much more, following their own research, the reasons behind some whole-school decisions and policies. 'It didn't mean you agreed but you understood the reasons why it was done' (Liz, School C). Interestingly, this greater realisation led to two paradoxical responses; on the one hand, staff were much more understanding of their line managers; on the other they were much more critical of them and their practice! They were both more critical *and* more tolerant. This was felt to be more empowering than frustrating, because it removed some of the helplessness felt in the face of the system. 'We are literally killing ourselves because of our inability to understand wholes' (Senge, 1991, p. 42). Already discussed in section 'Effects upon relationships in schools' in the previous chapter, it should be noted here that the increased awareness of the whole school included, for many teachers, a heightened consciousness of the centrality of students. Student perceptions were inevitably a focus for research in a number of research topics. Mel (School B) said:

> My eyes were opened as to what sort of deal the students were getting when I did my research into homework. I mean, this is a school where the teachers, including me, work hard, set and mark homework conscientiously but...! When I researched the students' end of it, I was brought back to my original question, which started out as a nice theoretical one: 'Why do we set homework?' I now realise, if I'm to be a manager, that I've always got to ask myself what the students will gain from this, whatever I'm doing.

Mike and Jo Fe (both of School A) also both discovered the importance of students and the dangers of ignoring their perceptions during separate research assignments into the school's special status. Being 'Grant Maintained' and perhaps more so a 'Technology College' is assumed perhaps to be a 'good thing' for staff, and of course for students, and assumed to be special. Mike's research into Technology College ethos produced for him all kinds of 'unexpected' reactions from students and 'they raised questions which we'd never even thought about and are still not ready to answer.'

What teachers had found was that whole-school development was really about what Senge (1991) describes as inter-relationships rather than linear cause and effect chains.

SENIOR MANAGERS' PERCEPTIONS OF THE SCHOOL'S CURRENT CULTURE

The views of seven senior staff, including two headteachers and two deputy head equivalents, were sought as well as those of three programme managers. The opinions of the headteachers of Schools A and B, where the research had been operating for some time, were very similar indeed. Both Richard (School A) and Tim (School B) were confident that their schools had developed or were developing a learning ethos which may be approximated to what Aspinwall and Pedlar (1997, p. 237) describe as an organisational learning style of:

> critical awareness [which] requires an open and questioning attitude to the organisation itself...Everything is open to critical questioning and analysis...Connections, underpinning values and ultimate purposes are explored in a serious attempt to understand the whole.

Both the heads referred, as do Aspinwall and Pedlar in this context, to the concept of double loop learning, i.e. questioning not so much whether adjusting practice to improve it is relevant but more whether it should be done at all or why it is done in the way it is (Argyris and Schon, 1981).

Tim (Head of School B) was clear that the school will 'genuinely improve through this kind of "owned" research'. His own view was that such activity helped to close the gap between educational research and actual practice and that 'through the 1980s we had people writing stuff about their research which no one in the classrooms, except those away on courses, actually read'. He felt that the intellectual progress that the researchers were gaining increased their job satisfaction and, for younger colleagues, would make them considerably better professionals in the years ahead.

Richard (Head of School A) was impressed by 'the quality of the scholarship displayed' and was clear that the debate in the staffroom now included much more talk about teaching and learning. Also, 'I hear conversations in corridors about "maybe I could do that as a piece of research". Staff talk avidly about what they are finding out and how it affects what the school's doing. This is not just with others in the group, but others in the department or year or whatever.'

Some of the work had been a 'revelation' to Tim and to Richard but also to the teachers themselves, particularly, Tim felt, as more teachers looked at issues 'through the eyes of the students now'. In School B, Tim gave one example that had changed his own views. Campion has a pastoral system based upon Houses.

> I had been dithering as to whether we should change to the Year system. The research into the role of the Head of House, House Teams and House ethos changed the climate of opinion engendered by the debate raised by the research. I became aware that, although there were some arguments for the Year system, there was an immense feeling for Houses, which swamped those. Since the pastoral system is based on ethos, the decision was made to stay with Houses and conflict was avoided.

He saw this as one of the values of in-house quality research, that it could address feelings and views in a 'measurable' way, making it easier for managers to make decisions not just based on the visible, tangible data 'so beloved of politicians today'.

Both headteachers believed that research developed a culture where issues ceased to be 'glib phrases' and became real. Tim used the example of 'students being responsible for their own learning'. What does it really mean? You can have a staff discussion at one level but when you have a piece of in-school research, showing what students actually do and what they feel they could do, it makes the discussion 'in touch with school practice'. Richard's main example had been described in a journal article concerning the rewards/sanctions issue at Lodge Park.

> It was clear from the data gathered that the school ethos was weighted too heavily towards the negative.
>
> (Middlewood and Parker, 1998, p. 54)

Faced with the evidence concerning punishments for poor homework, staff were able to debate the realities of the situation as a whole in the school and action followed (see Chapter 4).

Barbara (Deputy Principal at School C) made the same point. She felt that some of the issues presented by Senior Management as school priorities and therefore in development plans had become 'real' to the researchers. Boys' under-achievement became real when three people explored different aspects of boys' work and attitude at Samuel Whitbread. The research was specific and the work, for example, of Linda on boys and modern languages had, in the words of Kate (Assistant Principal) 'put out "tendrils" into all parts of the curriculum'. Linda's and Sue's work had shown that boys' under-achievement was an unhelpful phrase and raised the crucial questions of: Which boys? In which subjects? At what ages? From *which* contexts?

Morgan (1986) warned that 'organisational learning' required openness and self-criticism that is challenging to conventional management. In the three schools studied, the leaders accepted that by encouraging the research, this challenge would be part of the process. Kate (School C) was clear that the research group had a secure learning environment and they had to understand that there were no 'career threatening recommendations'! Healthy two-way debate, positive conflict and disagreement are part of the culture of a learning organisation. Liz (School A) said:

> Four years ago I would have said I was a teacher, now I would say I'm a professional. I understand about learning, the school, and have a picture overall about education. I won't just accept, blithely or complainingly, any new initiative from governments without question. I'll want to know its overall place and how it affects students.

When the two headteachers were asked whether the in-school research had affected their own roles, the replies were remarkably similar.

> It has made my job easier. People understand the issues so much more. I'm challenged more, which is exciting, and the research-based views keep the focus on what's actually happening in the school.
>
> Richard (School A)

> It's reduced my workload! More people have a whole-school perspective. I don't have to go to every meeting. If an unsubstantiated statement were made at a meeting, I know it would be challenged. Those meetings are more learning situations than they used to be.
>
> Tim (School B)

FACTORS AFFECTING THE DEVELOPMENT OF THE LEARNING CULTURE

No claim can be made that all schools involved in site-based research programmes can benefit equally in terms of impact upon culture. These three schools, all at different stages in such programmes, clearly feel they are making strides towards becoming learning organisations and that the programmes play important parts in this. Those case studies are offered as showing the possibilities inherent in site-based research where certain conditions prevail. Even for those schools, significant questions remain, notably concerning developments following changes in important personnel.

However, the work in these schools and awareness of other similar such situations lead me to suggest that the following factors are important in achieving a change in culture through school-based research involving a number of staff.

1. The initial support and *continued* encouragement of school leaders/ senior managers.
2. The willingness of these people to be challenged.
3. The enthusiasm and pastoral support of the school co-ordinator/tutor.
4. Careful and continuous presentation of the research group's work to the rest of the staff.
5. The support of the external tutor or consultant, particularly in ensuring quality of the research.
6. The careful co-ordination of research projects.
7. A plan for ensuring continuity of action when the programme reaches a natural end (e.g. end of a Higher Education course).

With these factors in mind, schools could see the establishment of a school-based research group as a powerful tool in their development as a learning school/organisation.

8

ENGENDERING CHANGE

David Middlewood

INTRODUCTION

This chapter examines some examples of changes that have occurred in schools where several teachers have carried out research projects. These changes relate to a recognition that new attitudes mean new approaches to policies, initiatives and their implementation, to new management programmes as well as to individual and team practices.

For the research assignments to have influence, they need often to be linked with other initiatives so that underlying principles may emerge. Looking at what some schools have done in terms of building upon the research group's approach, it is possible to see the work as potentially a powerful force for change. Evidence suggests that unless the work is reasonably widespread and offers ownership to as many people as possible, the impact may be lessened, especially as key people leave and/or support from 'above' wanes.

METHODOLOGY

The data for this chapter had been collected in the same way as for that in Chapter 6. Fourteen different schools in England in which several staff were engaged in accredited research assignments were used. A questionnaire concerning the effects of the research work was sent to the 107 teachers and 72 completed ones were received (a 67 per cent response rate) from across those schools. The numbers involved in the individual schools concerned ranged from 16 to two. Semi-structured interviews had been held with the researchers and with school managers at various stages. Additionally, such interviews were held with managers or research programme co-ordinators at six different schools during the spring and summer terms of 1998. In two schools from which questionnaires were received no interviews were possible and in three schools more than one manager was interviewed. See Table 6.1 (page 84) for a summary.

CHANGES IN ATTITUDE OF INDIVIDUALS THROUGH RESEARCH

An apparently simple realisation achieved through research mentioned by 50 per cent of teachers was that their own school was better than they thought it was! (Forty-nine per cent thought it was 'the same' as already perceived, one per cent thought it 'worse'.) One teacher said 'You always think your own school is not as good. You always think somewhere else is better.'

She referred to regular stories in the *TES* (*Times Educational Supplement*) about how 'good' schools had achieved 'this or that', and to the fact that, caught in the treadmill of everyday life in a busy school, it was easy to see what was wrong with your own. Carrying out structured research on a small-scale, focused way, enabled teachers to think otherwise in two ways. First, investigating an aspect of their own school's practice usually meant that much good practice was revealed and in fact, in general, people questioned were positive about far more things than they were negative about. Secondly, usually occurring in a later research assignment when the teachers had gained confidence in themselves as researchers, visits and data-collection in other schools also had the effect of making the teachers realise the value of what they had and the good practice in their own school. 'I used to think we were poorly off for resources' was one comment on a comparison even at the material level. Two different studies, based in two separate schools but each researching across a range of schools, found that management of part-time staff in their own schools had a number of features which the researchers deemed effective as being more present in their own schools. Staff in the other schools not only felt less valued but had less access to reading material, to training opportunities and fewer opportunities for discussion with their own line managers. In some areas, teachers reported that management practice in their own school, which they had assumed to be ineffective and inferior to elsewhere, was in fact the norm in other schools and that this was moreover seen as 'usual practice' by the staff in them. An example of this was when Sheila (Milton Keynes school) compared extra-curricular management across four similar schools; she found that the policy for supporting staff and students was the same in all four, and that staff at these schools found this satisfactory, not, as she had envisaged, that the practice at her school was inferior. This kind of comparison does not mean that particular management practices are effective or ineffective *per se*; what it does is offer the researchers a wider context for assessing the practice in their own school.

MacBeath (1998, p.127), in considering the change process in schools, describes how the appropriate opportunity 'led us directly to a group of staff ... who were eager to be involved and with an enthusiasm that eventually spilled out among their colleagues and proved a potent force for change.' He refers to Joyce's (1991) metaphor of the interconnected doors to describe the process of school improvement. This notion of the doors is appropriate and links with Townsend's (1971) reference to the fact that it is not possible to change people because that particular 'door' is locked from the inside. All managers can do is offer opportunities for those doors to be opened and, once they are, the interconnectedness referred to by Joyce (1991) becomes relevant. The point about a small change in attitude, such as indicated above, where a person simply realises that what is done at one's own place of work is as good as or better than what is done elsewhere, is that it can be the first inner door unlocked. An opening up of further changes in attitude is, at that point, a possibility.

A further and perhaps more significant realisation by some teachers doing research was that things were not set in the mould as they had assumed them to be. This is especially relevant to teachers (and probably employees in many organisations) who have worked in a particular school for a number of years. Our survey showed that, of the 36 teachers who realised that their schools were 'better' or 'much better' than they had realised, 31 had worked in those schools for more than eight years. As most people recognise, there is a danger in routines and established patterns in organisations in that, after a while, this institutionalisation of practices and also ideas and attitudes becomes reassuring and inevitably self-perpetuating. They do this because they appear to work, and when they do not it is easier to amend the operation rather than challenge the original assumption. This is the antithesis of 'double loop learning' (Argyris and Schon, 1981), at the heart of the learning organisation, discussed in Chapters 2 and 7.

Julian (Corby school) described the well-intentioned and 'normal' way of looking at an identified issue, in this case pupil motivation.

We set up a group of teachers, volunteers, enthusiastic mostly, who were interested. Out first meeting was good – lots of discussion and generally good thoughts about this issue. Second meeting, several people couldn't make it, so others lost heart. Third meeting we were still keen and thought it had been helpful to us individually. Eventually, it faded away. We didn't have a clear focus, didn't set ourselves a clear brief or seek one. We didn't have accountability, and so on. My own research assignment into pupil motivation was limited but I learned a lot more which I can apply in my own teaching and possibly in the department.

Julian said that he had learned that the established – and tempting – practice of setting up a group of interested enthusiasts to meet about the issue was not automatically productive. A focused individual investigation was, in his experience, more likely to yield results.

'I should have known better as a scientist!' he said. The working party notion had been normal practice in many ways. Julian, as a manager, is no doubt readier to challenge such accepted practice. It is not that such practice cannot work – clearly task groups can be very effective. It is more the issue of making an assumption that the 'normal' process is *the* way forward.

Sue (Bedfordshire school) described the situation and a realisation, after she had carried out a piece of structured and focused research into the identification of 'under-achieving boys'.

When you've been here a while, you tend to assume that things, at least the students, parents and so on, are basically the same as when you came. So, you say 'the thing about our students is … ' and 'our parents tend to … ' and so on. You base your teaching and management upon these. What I found out was that the attitudes were not the same as they used to be. After all, they aren't literally the same people. I had been stuck in a mind-set; *the kids had moved on* (my emphasis).

This is a powerful statement of a teacher with a door unlocked. Most of the time, MacBeath (1998, p. 128) suggests, teachers are too busy teaching to learn and management too busy maintaining the status quo to change. He refers to Covey's (1989) metaphor of the man sawing the tree who has been sawing for five hours and feels tired and less effective. When asked if he has stopped to sharpen the saw, he says he is too busy sawing. The opportunity to move away from the routine tasks and look at practice in a structured objective offered teachers chances to sharpen 'their tools for the job'.

It is perhaps useful to point out that research can prove disappointing to people when a cherished idea is challenged or at least 'unproved'. Ros (Wellingborough school) had become interested in the notion that pupils born in summer (June–August) performed less highly than those born in September and October, because of the way school entry is determined at the 31st August. An excellent piece of quantitative research, which also offered opportunities for links with achievement by gender, did not offer, however, evidence that was in anyway conclusive. Ros's work, however, was a valuable contribution to that debate and scotched any ideas that having a summer birth might offer an easy explanation for under-achievement.

BRINGING ABOUT SPECIFIC ORGANISATIONAL CHANGES VIA RESEARCH

Three examples are given of whole-school impact of particular areas of research.

(a) A Change in Ethos

A significant change in a school's ethos, described by the headteacher (Middlewood and Parker, 1998, p. 54) had its origins in a specific research assignment, negotiated with her tutor by Chris, one of the school's deputy heads and a student member of the school-based group. Chris had been concerned about the general emphasis on negativism in what was seen as a successful school in an area with considerable difficulties.

> I became particularly conscious that, in Year 7 (the intake year), students who apparently had not been in particular trouble at their primary schools seemed to be in a lot of detentions and causing problems. They were the same children, so was it our rules and regulations? Were we expecting too much? Or was it all just an impression I had, even though it was shared by some others? When we had had 'blitzes' upon bad behaviour or homework not being done, it seemed to result in a new structure of sanctions, for example, new ways of organising detentions. This seemed to be based on assumptions such as 'we must hit them hard at the beginning, get them into good habits – or at least out of bad habits.' But the number of detentions seemed to increase.

In hindsight, Chris was able to comment on the mind-set that had been established, but through her previous research assignments had realised that structured and focused research was needed. Her own research assignment led to a network of actions within the school, eventually drawing in all staff to a new approach – through, perhaps, a series of 'interconnecting doors'.

Stage One
Chris, through her normal links with the 'feeder' primaries, ascertained the normal regimes of sanctions and rewards that operated in the schools which supplied the majority of her school's intake, noting their different

kinds of 'merit and demerit' systems and also obtaining some (but limited) statistics of the extent to which rewards and punishments had been used in the last year. There was no attempt to track individual students' records 'for moral reasons' and the data were limited because of sensitivity to how individual primary schools might feel, but a clear picture emerged that the Year 7 students had all come from environments where 'there were more rewards than punishments'.

Stage Two

Given that her school did have a rewards system which was intended to place an emphasis on the positive, Chris's next research was to carry out a quantitative survey of the rewards given in all subject areas of the curriculum.

> I needed to find out if the rewards for achievement were given more in some areas than others, whether it was some teachers more than others, whether they were given more for some kinds of achievement than others.

Rather than focusing on Year 7, Chris's data covered the following two years also and produced a picture, perhaps unsurprisingly, of some inconsistency.

> One feature was that very few rewards – very few indeed – were given for homework being done well. Yet I knew that failure to do homework or not doing it properly was one of the major causes of students being in detention. It suggested that 'no homework equals bad', but not 'homework equals good' was in the eyes of students, perhaps. If there was a generalisation about staff from the data it was that younger, less experienced staff gave rewards to fewer students (not fewer rewards) than more experienced staff.

Stage Three

At this point, Chris's tutor pointed out to her that the research was taking on the scale of a major piece of work such as that of a Masters dissertation and sufficient existed already for an assignment! However, the momentum of interest generated by the research and in the data accumulated drew in other colleagues. Even a Head of Year who had genuinely expressed scepticism, but was also a member of the school-based research group, confirmed support for further investigation. The next action came from Chris's Deputy Head colleague, Ash, who volunteered to run a pilot scheme in alternative approaches to discipline in the classroom. It was important to use two parallel classes and two history groups in Year 9 were chosen that fitted the purpose. Over a period of five weeks, Ash taught the two classes similar curriculum content with similar instruction techniques and identical resources. With one group (A), however, he operated the current 'normal' school procedures concerning detentions and rewards for work in class and homework. With the other (B), he deliberately took the opportunity to praise more, to give out rewards more and to avoid the automatic use of detentions if no homework was produced.

At the end of the period, Ash and Chris were clear that the evidence was in favour of class B having produced better homework in some cases, equally good in many others, progress made by the students was greater and, significantly, Ash had enjoyed teaching B more than A, despite the difficulties he had found in switching mode. It was a small but influential additional piece of evidence.

Stage Four

Now assisted by several staff, Chris carried out a quantitative survey of detentions given across the whole of the age-group, 11–16 years. 'We looked at the frequency, numbers involved in each age group, and the reasons given especially noting those relating to homework.' The data collected was fascinating and for some staff the clearest evidence that collectively the school was weighted too heavily towards the negative.

> One thing that surprised me was that NQTs (Newly Qualified Teachers) were putting a disproportionate number of students in detention. They were young, keen and able teachers and we were giving them this message, obviously, that this is the way to get good work from your pupils. We hadn't intended to and we believed we were giving a positive message about the school. Other research had shown the NQTs thinking highly of the school as a positive and exciting place (which it is) but, unwittingly, *this* was being communicated.

Stage Five

Debate now took place at meetings of Year Tutor teams and of Senior Management as well as informal staffroom discussions.

Chris's research experience, along with that of other members of the school-based research group, led her to know that a more formal assessment of views was important. Semi-structured interviews were carried out with two Heads of Year, two NQTs and a small sample of parents concerning the ethos of the school, with particular reference to rewards and sanctions.

Stage Six

The Senior Management's proposals involved suggestions in two areas: staff training with regard to 'positive discipline', and the opportunity for the staff to propose a scheme of 'positive rewards'. John (Head of Year) and a colleague visited a conference on Assertive Discipline and his own investigations of its application in another school formed his own focused assignment. Staff task groups had a specific remit to introduce a scheme of rewards. A series of training sessions for all staff took place in the autumn term of 1997.

> The school's positive discipline scheme, with a sophisticated credit scheme linked to a formal high profile presentation of achievement certificates, was launched in January of this year (1998) and has made a significant impact on the school's culture: its emphasis has ceased to be used as a sanction and more students now remain behind after school to work.
>
> (Middlewood and Parker, 1998, p. 54)

Chris's research awareness makes her know that the change needs to be monitored, the impact examined and that this process will need to be equally structured. As well as being an example of how the research approach, supported by a group, is capable of being 'a potent force for change' (MacBeath, 1998, p. 127), it is one which stresses the importance of spreading change of shared values amongst people who work together – staff, students and parents too to some extent. These values also relate to wider social and moral values, the very ones expressed in the unease which Chris and a number of her professional colleagues had felt about the ethos, values above all held by them as decent members of that wider society.

(b) A Change in Policy and Practice

Homework is generally accepted – perhaps sometimes unquestioningly – as (i) the key interface between home and school and (ii) necessary to achieve high standards. It is not surprising therefore that in secondary schools it is an accepted part of practice and that considerable attention may be paid to ensuring that homework is set and that parents recognise they have a part to play in ensuring it is completed. None of this focus upon the effective *administration* of the homework guarantees anything about the quality of the learning that arises from doing the work. As Corno (1996, p. 27) says:

> Homework is a complicated thing ... The whole game of homework is extremely complicated, homework is not necessarily a uniformly 'good thing' for all students.

Teachers have therefore inevitably become interested in this as a topic for school-based research and several of them in the schools involved have investigated it as an assignment.

Mel's assignment in one Northamptonshire school had been given extra impetus by the national publications in England and Wales of proposals that minimum times for homework should be set for each pupil in primary schools as well as secondary schools. Her school had a typical statement on homework policy, on its setting and marking, its amount, its nature ('not every piece of homework will be written') and its purpose. It also operated a typical homework diary system, requiring parents' signatures. ('Typical', incidentally, was initially established by a collection of other schools' policy statements.)

Since teachers' views were regularly shared on the topic, Mel's research here focused on the perceptions of the other two key partners – the students and the parents. A questionnaire to a sample of students, another to the parents of that sample, some interviews with some of the students, including a group discussion and a scrutiny of some of the work actually produced by these students as homework, gave an insight into not only the operation but also the perceptions of those involved and how these affected what the students did. The data from the student and parent responses was illuminating. It showed clearly that:

- Parents were not clear what their part was in the partnership involved in homework (the signature in the diary was done dutifully but had little meaning for parents).

- Parents simply did not know how they could best help their own children.

- Students were not clear about the purpose of homework. Although the purposes were printed in the diary, most students admitted they did not read this part and it did not link with the work they were given to do.

These findings linked with the views of Corno (1996) that a number of assumptions that were made about homework, particularly the one about 'homework fosters discipline and personal responsibility' (*ibid.*, p. 28), had no foundation in practice.

The pieces of homework duly assessed that Mel scrutinised also showed that the feedback students were receiving from staff through their assessment gave mixed messages, including the fact that it was done at all being the most significant feature. Mel's school is one that has paid considerable attention to its relationships with parents, including investigating the role of parents as part of an evaluation of strategies for raising achievement in Year 11 (16-year-olds), and offering parents an opportunity to join evening seminars on parenting.

The Head and Deputy saw the importance and possible implications of the findings, especially in this context of effective relationships between home and school, being central to students' attitudes to learning. Some of the relevant reading (e.g. Bangs, 1996) had pointed to reports that pupils who like school tend to see the point of homework and pupils who dislike school attach less importance to it. Carole's research assignment into the ethos of her Northamptonshire school as perceived by Year 7s (intake year) students had also pointed to attitudes to understanding homework as being an issue for clarification with them.

Discussions with relevant staff followed and major changes have occurred. A homework diary is still used; a written document record has to be at the heart of regular communications between a teacher and between 20 and 30 homes, but there are differences.

- Parents are contracted to state their obligations in fulfilling their part of the partnership involved in using the diary as an effective tool for homework.
- Practical advice for parents as to how they can help their children as far as homework is concerned is now included.
- The purposes of homework are included in the diary, explaining to the students why it should be set.

The diary, therefore, is now intended to be a better reflection and aid to the mutual relationship between student, teacher and parent. Coleman (1998) sees this 'triad' as being the key to effective learning, following his extensive research with 10–14-year-olds.

This, plus some re-designing of the homework timetable, constituted a challenge to the established use of the diary, which was in danger, as in many schools, of becoming merely an administrative tool. It is likely that the context already existing in the school, in which the value of parental contribution to the 'learning partnership' was recognised, was significant in ensuring the research was utilised. A 'school improvement group', committed to further school-based research, will ensure structured monitoring and evaluation of the impact of these changes.

(c) Changes in Provision for Staff

Ian (Milton Keynes school) had responsibility for the management of all the non-teaching employees in his secondary school. These staff comprised more than 60 altogether (including clerical, technical, catering, previous management, cleaning and grounds personnel!). Having recently taken over the responsibility, Ian's examination of his job description revealed to him that:

> it was strong on functionalist aspects, pay, conditions and so on, but not much about managing them as people. In fact, the school had a general statement about valuing all people at the school for the contribution they make but some of these people just come in and out briefly and I wondered if they felt they belonged or, in some cases, whether anyone noticed their existence.

His reading, as with most teacher researchers, gave the stimulus for a specific focus. Literature was limited but reading Mortimore *et al.* (1994), the first major study of the use of associate staff in England and Wales following the introduction of Local Management of Schools (LMS), helped him reflect upon the entitlements of induction, appraisal and training which teaching staff had. He focused on induction, partly because he was involved in the recruitment and selection of associate staff and saw induction as the crucial next step and partly because 'frankly, appraisals had a bad press then and it wouldn't have been a good start'. He proposed investigating the feasibility of a school induction programme for associates, leading to proposals for its implementation. His own managers were sceptical so I fell back on the cost and quoted the 'The Industrial Society!' (Trethowan and Smith, 1984, p. 3):

> Anyone who doubts the necessity for such a programme should consider the economic cost of operating with a caretaker, technician or secretary whose knowledge skills or philosophy do not allow them to contribute effectively to their school.

Ian's reading concentrated now on induction in general and in reading about part-time staff in further education colleges, the issue of entitlement and the feelings of those people 'on the fringe' was something that Ian noted.

> It seemed that many of them didn't feel they had any right to induction or indeed felt they were worth helping.
>
> (Gartside *et al.*, 1988, p. 26)

The research assignment involved a study of the documentation (previous job descriptions) followed by a survey of all the current associate staff. The questionnaire used in the survey focused on three main areas, i.e:

- What form if any had induction taken for them as individuals?
- To what extent did they feel their contributions to the school were recognised?
- What would have been of value to them in first taking up the job?

When the data from the survey was collated, interviews with four key line managers were carried out (i.e. those with overall responsibility for premises, school office etc.).

> It was exhausting collecting the data. Some people, like cleaners, were very suspicious of the motives and with some I had to wait while they filled it in then and there, looking the other way! A 75 per cent response, however, was achieved and the data was revealing. Eighty per cent of associate staff felt they were not valued, their contribution was not recognised and they had been set on to the job with 'no understanding of what a school is like as an organisation'. The exceptions tended to be clerical staff. Most worryingly a majority of associate staff saw students as irrelevant, or a nuisance! The recognition that schools actually exist for students and that all of us, teachers, me included, depend on them for our jobs didn't seem to have been part of the thinking.

The interviews with line managers that followed were difficult, especially those who were responsible for 'contracted-out' services, such as cleaning.

> The cleaners were not directly employed by the school so the manager wasn't sure this side of things was any of my business. Progress was going to be much more difficult in some areas than others.

The programme proposed by Ian as a result of this research was ambitious and, when he evaluated it after one year, he recognised it as structurally unwieldy. It involved meetings with himself on the first day, introductions to key relevant personnel, and a talk about the school, its aims and achievements, and where it was felt they fitted in. Above all, they were given clear guidelines over relationships with visitors, teachers and students, including what action to take in relation to any discipline problems with the last group. Ian's recognition, a year later, was that the programme was too one-way.

> It didn't give the inductees enough opportunity to contribute. We were in control, talked at them, told them things. My proposals for the programme lost sight of one important thing the data was telling me. Some of these people didn't alter that. They needed to interact and begin to find their own worth as well.

However, the formal programme, flawed though it was, had significant influence. The fact of the need for its existence had drawn attention to the situation concerning associate staff in the school and related actions were taken. Heads of Year agreed that relationships between their cohorts of students and the cleaners in the specific areas were important. A part of the Personal and Social Education curriculum was devoted to their contribution and that of the canteen staff. This even involved interviewing particular personnel. All associate staff were introduced to the Year Group soon after appointment and all were invited to special Year occasions, such as celebration assemblies. Often attendance was not possible, but the invitations were made. Students know the names of all associate staff (formal surname or first name at the choice of the employee) and this, in the opinion of Year Heads, helped considerably in the care of the environment and in discipline issues. A research assignment by Sarah (same school), a year later, on the use of the physical environment, found that vandalism had decreased significantly in social areas.

> From my data, I concluded that the students were less likely to cause damage to an area when that area was somebody's, like Elsie's or Mary's, because that made it personal.

Other related actions included canteen staff joining Food Technology Classes to discuss diet and service and the Physical Education Department inviting grounds maintenance staff to seminars at which the importance of good facilities could be discussed between people all with a common interest in sport, 'not just teachers and people doing a job for them'.

Although much of the formal programme was abandoned by a new head teacher as being 'unnecessary', the changes described remain an intrinsic part of the way associate staff are inducted and treated.

Evaluation and improvements to formal staff programmes, such as induction, have proved valuable focuses for school-based research. Steve (Corby school), induction for teaching staff, and Lynda (Leicester school), induction for governors, were teachers whose research showed current provision was not meeting current needs of those for whom it was intended. Steve's research helped to move the induction programme towards meeting the needs of all those newly appointed to the school (recognised as a key need some years ago (SMTF, 1990)), while Lynda's research showed that the current LEA induction provision was wholly inadequate, because it was so detached from the actual school and fellow governors with whom the new governor would be working.

ISSUES FOR SCHOOL MANAGERS

Again, the research conducted here cannot produce clear evidence of pupil learning remaining at the centre. Whilst there is overwhelming evidence of commitment to this, and some research directly contributes to it, it is possible that in some schools a detachment of what is perceived as 'management' by classroom teachers may lead in these cases to a situation described by one teacher.

> We changed that system following the investigation, but it hasn't made any difference to what goes on in the classrooms with the students.

Although the majority (60 per cent) of teacher researchers were confident that the research had had a positive influence on student learning in the school, 30 per cent were also confident that it had not, apart from their own students, and those of a few colleagues. As stated elsewhere in this section, other factors may be overriding.

(a) Managing the 'Embedding' of Changes

Some of the proposed changes arising from school-based research may be short-lived; some cannot wholly be attributed to the research. In schools with only a small number of staff involved in research, teachers were more inclined to suggest as Sue (Essex school) did, 'some of my proposals in my research conclusion have been implemented. I can't claim responsibility because perhaps they would have happened anyway.' In schools where a larger proportion of the staff were involved, procedures have been adopted to ensure dissemination of the research and attempt an incorporation of it into the school's operations. Effective managers recognise that policies need to be accompanied by 'an effective strategy for reviewing the progress and impact of school policies and initiatives' (Ainscow *et al.* 1994, p. 12), and that the research assignments of a number of staff can offer effectiveness in this area, provided that there is:

- Widespread staff involvement in the processes of data collection and analysis.
- A clearly established set of 'ground rules' for the collection, control and use of school generated data.

(ibid., p. 12)

As Hopkins and Lagerweij (1996, p.86) insist, the research focus needs to be on the impact of policies:

not merely on implementation. It is all too easy to convince oneself that the school is being improved while, in reality, all that is occurring is a change of policies.

It is important for those managers to try to ensure the dissemination of the research and its findings rather than merely adopt or reject all apart of the findings because (a) the debates occurring through the process of dissemination will provide a check on the validity of the research process as well as its findings and (b) the ownership generated by the dissemination debates will be hugely significant in supporting the actual implementation of any real change in 'the collaborative setting' necessary (Fullan, 1985, p. 396).

i) Dissemination

In a Bedfordshire school, all the teachers involved in school-based research were required to report back to the whole teaching staff on a Professional Development Day, after the assignments had been submitted and assessed. Each person gave a presentation on what had been found and relevant study groups followed these up in focused discussion. The evaluations of that day showed, according to the Assistant Principal, 'an overwhelming positive view of the projects because they were based on a context everyone knew – our place!'

In a Plymouth school, teachers are each required to give a presentation to the Senior Management Team and, if possible, a representative of the governors.

In a Newport Pagnell school, all the research assignments are read by the Deputy Head, and the findings passed to what is seen as the relevant in-school body.

In a Wellingborough school, each teacher is required to report back to the section of the school of which he/she is a member (Department or Year depending upon the research topic).

In another Wellingborough school, the research project is a required item on the agenda for the next appropriate meeting of the section concerned.

None of these is unique and, in addition to the contribution to effective dissemination, they all have elements of accountability clearly in them. Since most of the schools have invested in the research through their support for the teachers' accreditation costs, senior managers wish to demonstrate effective use of resources to other staff as well as satisfy themselves.

One of the more permanent, and now quite commonly adopted, practices is for the written assignments to be bound and kept in staff libraries, rather in the way these are kept by university libraries. This not only offers prestige but helps the work become part of the school's references.

According to Miles (1986), summarised in Hopkins *et al.* (1994, p. 39), key activities in dissemination include:

- An emphasis on embedding the change within the school's structure; its organisation and resources.
- The elimination of competing or contradictory practices.
- Strong and purposeful links to other change efforts.
- Widespread use in the school.
- An adequate bank of local facilitators.

The survey findings suggest that a number of the schools have taken several of these steps, some others have taken at least a few of them. Four teachers have reported being approached as 'local facilitators' by other individuals who wanted something looked at or helped forward in their area. Some of the steps used by schools do indicate a strong desire not to let the impetus for school improvement given by the research be lost.

ii) Planning for the future

The schools which have seen research groups as powerful influences in the thrust for school improvement may seek ways of embedding the work so that even if an impetus is lost at any stage, e.g. through several key staff leaving, the movement is retained. One Northamptonshire school has established two staff groups. One is the School Improvement Group – mostly younger teachers likely to leave the school for promotion in due course – whose task is to feel free to look at anything which interests them, scrutinise it with rigorous research methods and submit to senior managers, 'to keep the school permanently on its toes and to motivate these particular staff' (Headteacher). This is paralleled by another

Strategic Planning Group, mostly longer serving staff in management roles, who take a longer term view of the school and between the two 'the aim is to balance staff needs – those who stay and those who go, value both, and use both for the school now and in the future' (Headteacher).

The Corby school described earlier has established its research group as a centre for an envisaged network of staff from local schools, hopefully building on its aim to be at the centre of a learning community and also widening the base for research. At the time of writing, it operates a group involving teachers from five different schools. However, two of the managers interviewed were vague about the future of research. Although enthusiastic about the current situation, neither has any precise plans for building the process of research into the plans for the future. Both 'hoped' and 'expected' that the impact would last, but did not offer ideas for ensuring that this was not dependent upon particular individuals. One in fact said 'I don't really know what will happen when (x) leaves'. It is reasonable to suggest that hope is unlikely to be sufficient!

(b) Keeping Pupil Learning at the Centre

The *relevance* of the research is critical in two ways; firstly, that it is seen as relevant by staff to the school's needs, and secondly that its topic and outcomes coincide with the central values that the school genuinely holds. This latter may be the most significant factor. Whilst findings from this work do not answer a number of questions, they do demonstrate the *potentially* powerful influence of multiple research by practitioners. The values held by the school may be the factor that instigates the research in the first place, of course. What happens to those values when challenged by the research may be the still largely unanswered question.

Stoll and Myers (1998, p. 9) emphasise that the change in the 'teaching and learning experience for pupils ... is where there are no quick fixes'. They argue that change here 'takes the greatest time because it involves intensive staff development, *new learning* [my emphasis] and, frequently, the need for a fundamental shift in beliefs about ways of working with pupils and their ability to learn' (*ibid.*). Several teachers reported looking anew at themselves and their students, not always directly because of the actual subject of the research, but because greater reflection was possible within a revised conceptual framework. Wendy's investigation into Post-16 Independent Learning at her Northamptonshire school had sent her back to reappraise her whole approach to teaching at Advanced Level:

> I cut the syllabus up into the bits where learning of a certain kind could occur, re-shaped the whole thing. They enjoy it more, I do too, and I'm certain they are now learning more independently of me.

All the management research assignments, including those concerned with the school's external relations, need to have this link with the learning and teaching of the students. As Chris B. and Chris W. (Corby school) pursued their research into parental involvement, examining satisfaction with parents' evenings and the management of 'stay-away' parents, it was important to remember at all times that the purpose of asking a parent on the evening whether they were satisfied with their experience, or asking a mother (in a supermarket!) questions about difficulties of getting into school was that, through the answers, might come a way of improving their children's learning. If this focus is lost, then there is the risk of changes occurring at procedural level, not at the one that matters.

Jackie (Programme Manager Northamptonshire school) felt this strongly.

> In the end, everything comes back to teaching and learning. That's what the school is ultimately judged by, that's what makes the daily job fulfilling or not for staff. Every outcome from research here eventually will have some implication for how we teach and learn here, and the better we do both, the better we'll get.

Again, the research conducted here cannot produce clear evidence of pupil learning remaining at the centre. Whilst there is overwhelming evidence of *commitment* to this, and some research directly contributes to it, it is possible that in some schools a detachment of what is perceived as 'management' by classroom teachers may lead in these cases to a situation described by one teacher: 'We changed that system following the investigation, but it hasn't made any difference to what goes on in the classrooms with the students.'

Although the majority (60 per cent) of teacher researchers were confident that the research had had a positive influence on student learning in the school, 30 per cent were also confident that it had not, apart from their own students, and those of a few colleagues. As stated elsewhere in this section, other factors may be overriding.

CONCLUSION

While the single teacher may be able to ensure that any changes occur as a result of a research project, this may be unduly dependent upon personal status or because the work coincided with the mood or need of the time. A group of teachers involved in school-based research *can* be a powerful force for change, especially if school management takes steps to ensure its embedding in school practice. Above all, what is embedded is the constant challenge to self and others. 'How do you know that?' becomes a natural response, not a simple denial. As a science teacher at a Leicester school said, 'We all know in the Science Department that split classes perform less well, I've got to find out properly. If I'm wrong, I'll be unpopular! But at least we'll know whether they really do or don't, or whether it's us that just don't like them.'

SECTION C:
SCHOOL IMPROVEMENT –
A RESEARCH-RICH ZONE

9

WHAT MAKES FOR EFFECTIVE RESEARCH IN A SCHOOL OR COLLEGE?

Marianne Coleman

INTRODUCTION

There are three aspects to the question posed in the title of this chapter. The first relates to the practicalities of actually carrying out the research, including consideration of the methods and tools that may be most suitable for small-scale research projects. The second aspect relates to those factors in the individual school or college that may support or hamper the carrying out of the research. These factors may include quite practical support, for example a financial contribution to a student's fees, or moral and psychological support expressed through the interest of senior management. A further dimension of this is the way that the wider culture may impact on the nature of the research that is being undertaken by the researcher practitioner. For example students in Chinese or Arab cultures might experience greater difficulties in obtaining access for research than students in the UK or North America.

The third aspect, the effectiveness of the research in terms of its impact on the school or college, will largely be addressed in Chapter 10 where we consider the role of the practitioner researcher and the relationship of such research to school or college improvement. However, the present chapter ends with an overview of the impact of their research, reported by the 41 MBA students who responded to a questionnaire issued by the authors.

THE REALITY OF CARRYING OUT PRACTITIONER RESEARCH IN A SCHOOL OR COLLEGE

All assignments and dissertations completed as part of the course leading to the MBA in Educational Management contain an investigation into an area of management and therefore require students to undertake a piece of small-scale research. Students are encouraged to use the research tools or methods that are most appropriate to their defined purpose, and to justify their choice.

In 1998, a survey of current students who had completed two or more assignments was undertaken asking them to complete a questionnaire in respect of one or more of their assignments. The questions related to:

- the choice of research methods;
- problems encountered with the research;
- strengths of the research method used;
- support from the school or college;
- the nature of recommendations arising from the research;
- personal and professional benefit to them as individuals;
- benefit to their organisation arising from the research.

One hundred students were approached, and 41 responded. Their responses provide much of the data for this chapter. Students were asked to send a copy of their chosen assignment with the returned questionnaire, something of a demand on busy professionals who are also undertaking a part-time distance learning Masters level course.

It may well be that the students who felt moved to respond were those for whom the experience of writing assignments had been largely positive. One student, in an addendum to his responses to the questionnaire stated that:

> I think your survey neglects how enjoyable it is to study for this MBA. Researching into one's school (or college) is of itself very, very interesting. The literature search helps put that aspect you have chosen into a wider context and it's great to know that these issues are elsewhere too, and to find echoes in the work of others.

Over 75 per cent of the responses indicated that the choice of subject for their assignment was made to meet the needs of both the individual and their institution. In the case of the remainder of the students, half made the choice on their own behalf and half on behalf of their school or college.

RESEARCH TOOLS – CHOICES, PROBLEMS
AND STRENGTHS

Johnson (1994) differentiates between 'research approaches' – 'the main ways in which research can be tackled' (p. 13) – and 'research tools' – 'the means by which different approaches to research are operationalised'. She includes amongst the research approaches: surveys; case studies; documentary research; the experimental approach and non-reactive research. To this list could be added action research, defined by Cohen and Manion (1994, p. 186) as being a:

> small-scale intervention in the functioning of the real world and a close examination of the effects of such intervention.

Amongst the range of research tools, Johnson (1994) includes: questionnaires; interviews; observation; the use of records or other documents and the use of diaries as a research tool.

The students' questionnaire responses related to the practicalities of carrying out their research and to the associated difficulties and successes. Therefore most of their responses related to the actual research tools that they had used rather than dealing with what Johnson (1994) terms the 'research approaches'.

Table 9.1 *Use of research tools in one chosen assignment*

	Per cent of students using
One research tool	27
Two or more research tools	73
Questionnaires	78
Interviews	49
Documentary analysis	32
Observation	12
Other	15
Number of responses	**41**

In addition, four students specifically stated that they had used an action research approach. Documentary analysis and observation were always reported as being used in association with other tools, either interviews or questionnaires. Amongst the category 'other' were focus groups, telephone interviews, use of quality education checklist, SWOT analysis and the use of an external consultant to carry out interviews, all examples of the use of a specific technique which could be considered broadly as lying within the category of either interviews or questionnaires.

REASONS FOR THE CHOICE OF RESEARCH TOOL

1. Questionnaires

There were several reasons given for the use of the most popular research tool, questionnaires. The most common reasons related to the need to collect data from a large group. One student undertaking a SWOT analysis on marketing in the Hong Kong Academy of the Performing Arts commented that he 'wanted to survey opinion in a large group (155 students)'; another conducting a study of staff morale in a rural secondary school, that 'it was a means of targeting the entire staff'.

Further reasons for using a questionnaire were that staff and sometimes pupils were used to completing questionnaires and that it gave time and space for respondents to consider their answers in privacy and at their leisure. Questionnaires might be:

> intended to provide middle managers with an opportunity to reflect on their perceptions of their own role ... and to consider their development needs,

and in addition:

> It is easier to answer a questionnaire than to be interviewed by the Principal!

2. Interviews

Interviews were generally chosen in order to get a more detailed response than might be obtained from a questionnaire:

> It [interviewing] is a powerful way to gain insight into educational issues through understanding the experience of the individuals whose lives constitute education.
>
> (Seidman, 1991, p. 7)

However, there were examples of quite specific needs, in one case: 'to find out if they had ideas I had not thought of' where a student was attempting to identify the characteristics of an effective headteacher, preparatory to drawing up a person specification for the appointment of a new head for an International School. A student who is a headteacher of a South African school used interviews rather than questionnaires in assessing the image of the school because:

> the respondents comprise largely illiterate people. The interview enabled me to communicate with them orally. This method enabled me to probe for more specific answers, observe non-verbal behaviour.

3. Documentary Analysis

Documentary analysis and observation are research tools that tend to be used as supplementary to either interviews or questionnaires or both, often within a case study approach. They may be used to obtain background material and derive research questions. One student attempting to produce a development plan for pastoral care in a secondary school used documents to 'investigate the history of the school and the evolution of pastoral care arrangements'. Another, undertaking the development of a marketing strategy in an independent school, made use of a report undertaken some years earlier by a consultant.

The use of documents may also be to discover the official view of school aims or to identify policy statements, or alternatively documents might provide an official record of events, such as a governors' meeting. Documentary analysis relies on the use of available printed or written data, although the term may be extended to include non-written documents such as films and photographs. Robson (1993, p. 274) lists as documents a very wide range of general documents including:

> minutes of meetings;
> letters, memoranda, etc.;
> diaries;
> speeches.

However, he comments that in studies of schools and colleges, documents could include:

> written curricula;
> course outlines and other course documents;
> timetables;
> notices;
> letters and other communications to parents.

Inspection reports could also be added to this list.
Documentary analysis is often used as a means of triangulation:

> Triangulation may be defined as the use of two or more methods of data

collection in the study of some aspect of human behaviour.

(Cohen and Manion, 1994, p. 233)

The technique of using more than one type of research enables the researcher to study the same subject from more than one point of view, thereby establishing greater confidence in the findings.

Examples of the use of documentary research as triangulation include the review of specific documentation as part of an evaluation of the pastoral care and guidance system in an Hong Kong School, and a review of all records of meetings relating to the introduction of a special education unit to a school in Sydney, Australia. In both cases the researcher had used interviews and questionnaires as the main source of data.

4. Observation

The ways in which observations are used were rarely specified in the survey of MBA students, although comments were made about the 'accuracy' and 'directness' of the evidence. However, a student interviewed during the course of the preparation for this book gave a detailed account of the use of observation for her dissertation on the subject of the accountability of middle managers. The observation was of a governors' committee meeting and the account identifies the importance of systematically observing a limited range of relevant details, in this case the extent and number of contributions to the discussion:

> I had to justify covert observation of a Governors' Curriculum Committee meeting, if I'd told them beforehand it would have altered the situation. I was used to taking minutes and doing appraisal involving classroom observations and used to doing timings. I felt it would not be possible to categorise behaviour or interactions but I timed the amount and number of contributions. I tabulated them and categorised them according to agenda items, in each case how long, and how many times, each person spoke. It showed that the Head and Chair had read in great detail before the meeting but other governors were rarely speaking and were not well prepared (there were 94 pages of curriculum material to read!).

In educational management, observation is most likely to be used in respect of meetings, and whilst specific objectives will depend on the purpose of the research, Williams (1984) suggests that a starting point for observation might be either the issues covered or the people involved.

(a) For each issue in turn:
  – who speaks on that particular issue?
  – for how long?
  – what is the nature of their contribution – particularly in helping to achieve the objectives of the meeting?

- what helped progress on the issue?
- what hindered progress on the issue?

(b) For each person in turn:
  - what did they contribute to the discussion?
  - what was the nature of their contribution?
  - how did they help in achieving the purposes or objectives of the meeting?
  - how did they hinder the achievement of purposes or objectives?

(Williams, 1984, pp. 209–210)

PROBLEMS AND STRENGTHS OF SPECIFIC RESEARCH TOOLS

The majority of comments by the students using questionnaires related to response rates. Poor response rates were sometimes due to the perception on the part of the respondent that the questionnaire was over-long, sometimes to resentment at what may be seen as 'another administrative burden imposed from above'.

Some specific problems included the difficulties of getting responses from parents where the questionnaire was delivered by students – 'I realised some would not get home' – and the difficulty in getting responses from a school other than the teacher's own, where loyalty might ensure a good result. A teacher who carried out a comparative survey of two schools on the subject of total quality management reported an 'uneven response rate from the two schools'.

On the other hand a larger number of students using questionnaires reported good response rates, excellent where they had been physically able to give out questionnaires and in some cases collect them back in.

Problems with design and with ambiguous questions were sometimes linked with lack of piloting. Certainly the reporting of both problems and strengths identifies the importance of planning ahead in the construction of questionnaires. Johnson (1994) comments on the importance of two issues in questionnaire design:

> the respondent's need to understand the questionnaire and find it relevant to his or her knowledge, experience, and expertise; and the researcher's need to try out the questions before sending out the questionnaire in its final form.
> (p. 39)

One student, investigating the effectiveness of a problem solving team, regretted that he included a five-point scale: 'a 1–5 rate-alternative allowed a response of 3, the non-committed line', and that 'about 50 per cent of the staff found two of the questions too ambiguous and did not answer them'.

Planning and design also relate to the ease of analysis of the responses. One student investigating middle management styles commented that the questionnaires 'though time-consuming to construct were easy to complete and analyse'.

While others commented that 'the questions sometimes provoked a range of responses which were difficult to summarise/categorise'; 'the more "open" questions in the questionnaire proved difficult to incorporate reliably in the findings'.

An additional strength of the questionnaires is the benefit of anonymity, particularly where criticism of individuals may be involved. In reference to an investigation of staff perceptions of leadership, one student commented that questionnaires 'allowed staff to raise their "voices" whilst remaining anonymous'.

Strengths and problems were also reported in respect of the use of interviews. The main strength was seen to be the flexibility of the semi-structured approach and the valuable qualitative data that may emerge. A student investigating the development of a marketing strategy in an independent school commented that 'interviewees did digress and make valuable points that I had not anticipated'.

A student investigating the role of the curriculum manager said that 'respondents preferred to talk in a semi-structured interview and as a result provided a lot of useful data. A lot of frank discussion which provided valuable whole-school insights.' In addition, one student noted that the actual process of interviewing can be helpful: 'it is an ideal way of valuing staff and building relationships.'

Difficulties with interviews arose from the danger of manipulation by either the interviewer or the interviewee, and most of all from the time implications associated with carrying out the interviews, including getting agreement from the interviewees on the accuracy of the record of the interview and for the time taken to transcribe tape-recorded interviews. One student reported that transcriptions took her eight hours to complete, but transcription can take much longer. Although estimates of the time involved vary considerably and must depend on the amount of detail required. Johnson (1994, p. 50) reports that 'one hour of recorded interview requires nine hours for transcription and checking'.

Advantages of the use of documentary analysis included for a new member of staff 'the opportunity to find out more about the school', but the main advantage of documentary research may be for those who find direct research access difficult for cultural or micro-political reasons.

Documentary analysis is an example of unobtrusive or non-reactive research. Unlike questionnaires or interviews, documentary research does not make demands on people, and the sources themselves are not affected by the fact that they are being used for the enquiry. Whereas it may be difficult to access a senior manager for interview about strategy in a college, it may be possible to access the strategic plan relatively easily. Most documents were not produced with any intention that they might be used for research. However, educational sources such as minutes, reports, prospectuses and staffing information, although created for purposes unconnected with any research, may provide very valuable data.

Some of the problems reported raise issues of ethics in relation to research. Teachers or lecturers researching in their own institution may have to be particularly sensitive to issues such as taking the time of their colleagues in the research process and maintaining their anonymity when disseminating the research outcomes. This may be particularly difficult in a small institution. The insensitive or unscrupulous use of research findings on the part of the researcher, or potentially on the part of the senior management team, indicates the possibility of using research data for micro-political ends. The researcher and those supporting site-based practitioner research should therefore aim to maintain the integrity of the researcher and apply the highest ethical standards to the research in all its stages.

SUPPORT FOR PRACTITIONER RESEARCH WITHIN THE SCHOOL OR COLLEGE

The students who responded to our request for information about their research reported overwhelmingly that they had received support from their school or college. Over 50 per cent of the comments specifically related to support offered by the senior management. However, the extent of the support reported was variable. In some cases, the research was completely integrated into a larger school initiative with the full backing of senior management. In a study of the process of budget decision-making at a secondary school, the student reported that:

> This was the first investigation following the appointment of a new headteacher. She was involved in the early stages of the planning and was always the main 'audience' for the assignment. The work was therefore closely linked to school development.

Most of the comments were completely positive, but there were those that indicated some ambiguity on the part of the senior management, particularly when the research outcomes were not necessarily welcome:

> The head approved of study although was not keen on the outcomes.

For all the work I did and am doing the head is supportive – he condones what I do – but is not keen to read or discuss.

In some cases neutrality from senior management was welcomed: 'I had no interference at all from the head (this was an advantage!).'

Support was also reported from members of the teaching staff, who appeared particularly responsive where the research investigation was relevant to their needs or where the work for the MBA is seen as relevant to the progress of the school or college. Reporting on an evaluation of the effectiveness of middle managers, one student commented that: 'all were keen to be involved as it was presented to them as an opportunity for reflection leading to improvements.' Another student reported that 'the teachers were usually very willing to participate in the study and had a lot to offer in the way of suggestions as to how to best carry out the survey'.

However, the extent of the support did vary: 'the staff were quite helpful although I expected more. I could not run after or remind the staff a second time.'

Governors too were identified as supportive: 'I was given time at Governors' meetings to introduce and feed back on the investigation. The Headteacher and Chair of Governors gave it their full support, and were among those interviewed.'

About a quarter of those responding reported that they received some form of financial support, varying from payment for printing and paper expenses to partial or full payment of fees. In some cases students have also been given time and allowed release to undertake investigations or to write up the assignment. Other comments related to having clerical support and to being given access to information of a privileged nature. One fortunate student reported that he was granted 'access to everything as required and the time provided for the research process; all resources provided by the school'.

Only three students commented on a lack of support, indicating that the research was unlikely to have any impact:

'no support from headteacher, did not give weight to my research, in spite of it being related directly to the needs of the school. This in turn meant some teachers did not value in-school research.'

THE IMPACT OF NATIONAL CULTURE ON PRACTITIONER RESEARCH

The majority of the students who responded to the survey reported positively in terms of both the process and the outcomes of their research.

However, practitioner research may face particular difficulties that are related to the cultural norms of their society. There is some limited evidence of this in the cases illustrated elsewhere in this book. The investigation of the influence of gender on management roles by a primary school head in London was partly inspired by the fact that there is a disproportionately large number of male primary heads, an indication of the tendency for power to be located with men, even where there is a predominantly female teaching force. The male and female headteachers who were interviewed were able to undertake a sophisticated analysis of the impact of gender on the role of the primary headteacher. However, the study of role stress among Druze women teachers indicated the extent to which women in that society were still expected to carry out their traditional family role. There simply were no women managers in the school. Both these investigations are reported in Chapter 3.

Differences in culture will affect the subject matter of research but may also affect the attitudes to research and the ways in which research may be carried out. Vulliamy *et al* (1990) comments on the preference for quantitative research in developing countries:

> a recent survey of educational research environments in the developing world suggest that, with the isolated examples of a few countries such as Columbia, the use of qualitative research strategies is still relatively under-developed.
>
> (p. 16)

The heavy reliance on qualitative methods in Western research on educational management may therefore pose particular difficulties for student researchers whose academic training has not been within a Western culture, and whose background may lead them to think of research purely as the collection of statistics. Traditionally the collection of research data on education has been quantitative and has been for the use of policy makers (Ross and Mahlck, 1990). The corollary of this may be a lack of the tradition of individual research within a school or college context.

In some societies, a particular difficulty for practitioner researchers may be a tradition of respect for superiors, that makes investigation, with its implication of criticism, a sensitive issue. Hofstede (1980) refers to the difference in the power distance ratio, or the extent to which inequality is accepted in Western and Eastern countries. It is likely to be difficult for a teacher or lecturer to interview their superiors and investigate and suggest recommendations for change in a society such as Hong Kong where:

> high power-distance seems to predispose them to following and respecting the authority and power of a strong leader to whom they look for direction and structure;

and:

rank-and-file teachers often see participation as a privilege granted from above rather than as a right.

(Dimmock, 1998, p. 372)

However, Dimmock does note that the rapid pace of change in Hong Kong does mean that younger generations hold different values to 'their more traditional parents and grandparents' (*ibid.*, p. 375).

A further cultural difficulty, allied to that of respect for those in authority, is a diffidence about the publication of research findings expressed by some of those who did complete and return the questionnaire.

It is likely that the majority of students who responded to the survey were those who did have something positive to report. It has already been noted that almost all indicated that they had received some kind of support from their school or college. The letter accompanying the questionnaire asked the students to pick an example of an assignment to evaluate in terms of the benefits to themselves and their organisation. It is therefore not surprising that the students were able to list a large range of recommendations that they had made and a list of adopted recommendations that was only a little shorter.

RESEARCH RECOMMENDATIONS AND THEIR ADOPTION

Despite the fact that most of the recommendations mentioned in the questionnaires appear to have been adopted, problems were reported where the implementation of the recommendations was dependent on the will of the Senior Management Team. One student, although positive about some of her recommendations, commented that 'from a whole-school point of view it is more difficult as the SMT are resistant to suggestions'.

The indications from the survey were that the recommendations made following the small-scale research investigation were more likely to be adopted when they were relatively short-term and practical, particularly when they were directly controlled by the person who had undertaken the research.

A student, whose assignment was entitled 'Towards an effective school development plan for pastoral care in an 11 to 16 school', reported that:

The implementation and short-term planning recommendations have been adopted. The long-term considerations have not been as successful. Staff training, although present, is limited due to financial restraints.

Another student working on a marketing strategy reported the adoption of a range of practical recommendations including:

1. Homework club started; 3 p.m. daily.

2. Years 6 and 7 reminded of behavioural policy.

3. Parents charter started.

One student investigating the deployment, development and integration of non-teaching staff was able to report the decision to involve associate staff in specific ways:

Associate staff are increasingly involved in training on school INSET days. An associate member of staff has been co-opted on to the school governors.

Recommendations arising from an assignment on the role of the NQT mentor in the secondary school were fully adopted, but most of the changes were in the form of written documentation:

A more tightly structured/managed induction and mentoring policy is in place for all staff; a better and earlier 'matching' system is in place. Mentors have 'job descriptions'.

The evaluation of the implementation of recommendations through a questionnaire can be no more than a snapshot, and it would be necessary to carry out further evaluations at a later stage in order to see how embedded the changes actually are. However, students reported benefits from the research both to themselves and to their schools in terms of an increased access to accurate information. This could have wide ranging longer term effects which are likely to inform future action and increase the likelihood of planning and decision-making being based on data derived from in-house research. An example is: 'a more fully informed SMT on TQM'. Similarly, the principal of St Malachy's College quoted in Chapter 3 referred to basing planning on data collected in the school, rather than 'wishful thinking'.

There is considerable evidence from the questionnaire responses that individual students have benefited in terms of increased understanding and confidence and feel better able, as a result, to apply for promotion. It would seem likely that their increased expertise and understanding would be to the benefit of their present and future schools and colleges:

I have become a more reflective senior manager and I understand organisational processes better.

I now have a broader knowledge of the area which will prepare me for a post as a Deputy Head. I am more aware of the perspectives of others in the school.

It has been of huge benefit in taking over as Head of a similar type of school. I have implemented several of the main points raised...

As a comparatively new first-time Principal I have developed (a) self confidence (b) awareness of the problems perceived by colleagues (c) confidence and the dedication of colleagues.

Such benefits are reported in relation to the classroom, as well as in respect of senior management roles:

Benefits have been in terms of my professional development and the maths curriculum as I am now tackling changes differently and finding them more successful.

I was surprised to find how badly I had communicated the nature of the course to the students.

However, research can be revealing in a number of ways and one comment, relating to an assignment on the effectiveness of an interviewing team, was that it had been 'very, very instructive – it shows how badly a team can work together'. As a result there were no recommendations:

None – I deemed the report too damning – too negative and have hidden the report from *all* the staff.

The outcomes of research reported in the questionnaire were largely very positive, but the data are not triangulated. However, the data reported in Chapters 2 to 8 are derived mainly from our own case study schools and colleges, where a number of interviews took place in addition to the use of questionnaires. This in-depth research helps us to identify some of the wider institutional and cultural issues that are likely to affect the success or failure of practitioner research in schools and colleges and, in particular, how this might relate to school and college improvement. The implications of the case study research supported by some additional data from the questionnaires are reported in Chapter 10.

10

CONCLUSIONS

Marianne Coleman

The preceding chapters have introduced the concept of practitioner research in the context of institutional improvement and have shown examples of practitioner research in action. These examples indicated some of the reasons why the practitioners embarked on research, the methods that they used and what they hoped to gain for themselves and for their organisation. Research undertaken by individual practitioners in schools and colleges is generally intended to have some effect on the organisation. Some consideration has been given to what factors in the school or college may promote the research, and this final chapter is largely concerned with the outcomes of practitioner research and the ways in which they might relate to school and college improvement.

In considering the nature and impact of practitioner research through the examples, we also attempt to explore the relationship of practitioner research to the research paradigms and criticisms of educational research introduced in Chapter 1.

THE RELATIONSHIP OF PRACTITIONER RESEARCH TO IMPROVEMENT AND EFFECTIVENESS

In Chapter 1 some of the main differences between research into effectiveness and research into improvement were outlined. These included the emphasis on outcomes as opposed to processes, looking for a direct effect on student achievement as opposed to an indirect effect, having a 'top down' approach as opposed to a 'bottom up' approach, an emphasis on quantitative rather than qualitative research, and the built in expectation of change in school and college improvement.

Table 10.1 *The separate traditions of school effectiveness and school improvement*

School Effectiveness	School Improvement
Focus on schools	Focus on individual teachers or groups of teachers
Focus on school organisation	Focus on school processes
Data driven, with emphasis on outcomes	Rare empirical evaluation of effects of changes
Quantitative in orientation	Qualitative in orientation
Lack of knowledge about how to implement change strategies	Concerned with change in schools exclusively
More concerned with change in pupil outcomes	More concerned with journey of school improvement than its destination
More concerned with schools at a point in time	More concerned with schools as changing
Based on research knowledge	Focus on practitioner knowledge

(From Reynolds *et al.*, 1993, p. 44)

Although one of the factors listed in relation to school effectiveness is the focus on the school, more recent studies are tending to focus on the classroom level factors that directly affect learning and achievement, whilst school improvement tends to be concerned with a multiplicity of factors including parents and communities where the impact on student achievement can only be indirect.

> There is a lot of improvement going on which has little relevance for effectiveness because it does not aim at enhancing student outcomes at all.
> (Creemers and Reezigt, 1997, p. 402)

THE LINKS WITH EFFECTIVENESS

The above quotation from Creemers and Reezigt may be something of an over-statement, certainly in one school (Chapter 8) it was strongly felt that learning and teaching were central to all research projects:

> In the end, everything comes back to teaching and learning. That's what the school is ultimately judged by, that's what makes the daily job fulfilling or not for staff. Every outcome from research here eventually will have some implication for how we teach and learn here. (Middlewood, p. 135)

Following an assignment intended to evaluate the impact of a whole-school initiative to enhance the effectiveness of teaching and learning, one student commented on the use of the research findings which make a clear link between school improvement processes and effectiveness outcomes:

> As a tool to work better for school improvement. We have the information on which to work if we want to improve the assessment mark.

However, it may be that the possibility of improvement is 'crowded out' by what is seen as the imperative of school effectiveness. In the case of the secondary school teacher reported in Chapter 2, his research on the induction and mentoring of new teachers was seen as 'peripheral' to the core activity of teaching and learning and not encouraged, although the member of staff responsible for induction did comment on the usefulness of the research which had led her to a deeper understanding of the concept and purpose of mentoring.

In some cases, outcomes of research could be seen as relevant to effectiveness, where this is specifically defined as relating to raising student achievement. Several of the school- and college-based research projects were designed to enhance the curriculum and its delivery and directly effect learning: an investigation into Post-16 Independent Learning (Chapter 8); the development of the learning resource centre at Rugby College; and the support of learners inside and outside the classroom at Loughborough College. Similarly the changed curriculum for electronics in the college in the United Arab Emirates moved the focus from teaching to learning (Chapter 5).

There may be other direct links between aspects of the research reported in this book and effectiveness. One aspect of the school effectiveness movement has been to attempt to identify those common factors that may be found in effective schools. The following is a list which reflects international research and inspection evidence and, summarising mainly British research literature, provides a list of 11 key factors associated with effective schools.

1. Professional leadership   Firm and purposeful
   A participative approach
   The leading professional

2. Shared vision and goals   Unity of purpose
   Consistency of practice
   Collegiality and collaboration

3. A learning environment   An orderly atmosphere
   An attractive working environment

4. Concentration on teaching   Maximisation of learning time
   and learning   Academic emphasis
   Focus on achievement

5. High expectations   High expectations all round
   Communicating expectations
   Providing intellectual challenge

6. Positive reinforcement   Clear and fair discipline
   Feedback

7. Monitoring progress   Monitoring pupil performance
   Evaluating school performance

8. Pupil rights and responsibilities   High pupil self-esteem
   Positions of responsibility
   Control of work

9. Purposeful teaching   Efficient organization
   Clarity of purpose
   Structured lessons
   Adaptive practice

10. A learning organization   School-based staff development

11. Home-school partnership   Parental involvement

(Sammons *et al.*, 1995, p. 8)

Without going through each of these individually it can be seen that many, if not all of the factors have been enhanced by the research investigations reported in this book. One example is that indicated by David Middlewood in Chapter 6, where he comments on the increased understanding of learning experienced by the teachers in their own student role and, resulting from this, their increased expectations of their own students. Another example is in the deliberate attempt to change a negative to a positive student ethos, reported in Chapter 8, thus promoting positive reinforcement and increased student self-esteem.

THE LINKS WITH SCHOOL AND COLLEGE IMPROVEMENT

Whilst the schools and colleges reported in this book may exhibit aspects that are equated with effectiveness, and the research may lead to the promotion of effectiveness, practitioner research can more easily be identified with school and college improvement. This identification can be seen in terms of the focus on the practitioner instigation of research, on groups of teachers working together, attention to processes rather than outcomes and, most of all, through the fact that the research is purposeful and carries the implication of change.

The focus on change is an intrinsic aspect of improvement as is the role of the practitioner in bringing about change. Huberman (1993, pp. 41–43) distinguishes 'instrumental effects' which are 'changes in tools or methods of daily work; changes in policies or practices at a more institutional level' and 'conceptual effects' which are 'clear conceptual connections between the main findings of the study and the informants' work situation'. The research projects reported by the researcher practitioners through the questionnaires appear to indicate that these different levels of change may occur as a result of the research:

1. *Small-scale change* – an individual undertakes a piece of research in an area where he or she has some jurisdiction and is therefore able to act, often in a quite practical way, to implement recommendations based on the findings. The outcome could be termed 'instrumental'.

2. *Potential long-term change* – research produces information which may impact on the individual researcher and on those to whom the research findings are disseminated. It is probable that such data may inform future action and may bring about 'conceptual effects'.

3. *Whole-school or college change* – the researcher has the active support of others in the school or college, the backing of senior management is particularly relevant. This may be as part of a whole-school initiative. Here the outcome is likely to be 'conceptual' in Huberman's terms.

Glatter (1988) considers that such differences of scale, size and scope can all be encompassed within the term 'school improvement' (see Chapter 1).

RESEARCH INVESTIGATIONS AND CHANGE

Small-Scale Change

Many examples of this first type of institutional effect emerge from the survey data. Individual site-based researchers comment on changes resulting from their research that may or may not be embedded in the school, but, at least in the short term produce benefits to themselves, their teams and their teaching:

> Meetings are much more constructive.

> Pro-forma devised based on my research to ascertain tutors' development needs/INSET re pastoral care.

> Exit interviews are conducted.

Other such changes may include the production of handbooks and policies.

Potential Long-Term Change

The impact of fresh information can lead to insights or may promote reflection leading to future action. Commenting on the benefits of their research projects, individual students completing the questionnaire identified learning outcomes that had the potential to lead to change:

> I have become a more reflective senior manager and I understand organisational processes better.

> The process provided considerable clarity as to the place of pastoral care and guidance in the school.

> a realisation that finance in a school is only significant in terms of its impact on the quality of teaching and learning.

> I have an improved insight into the wishes and values of parents.

An example of the type of research which produces data that may inform future action including style of management is the research on gender undertaken by a primary school and a special school headteacher and reported in Chapter 3. For these researchers benefits came from the exploration of leadership style and increased self-knowledge, and in the case of the female headteacher an increase in confidence.

In the case of the researcher in a tertiary college (Chapter 2) the actual purpose of the research was to provide information on staff morale and motivation that was intended to be useful for the middle management team:

> the findings did inform ongoing debate and as such contributed to the change process.
>
> (Lumby, p. 30)

It was also felt that perceptions could now be underpinned by the actual data that the researcher had derived relating to staff morale and motivation rather than uninformed supposition.

In a different way, those teachers who worked at schools where a number of teachers were involved in research felt the benefit of the 'accumulated wisdom' (Middlewood, p. 86), even suggesting that the collected assignments would be the first thing to consult, if they were called for interview.

Whole-School or College Change

It is the third type of research that is likely to have the most impact. When the research project is carried out by a member of the senior management team, or alternatively has the backing of the senior management team, the recommendations arising from the research appear to have a good chance of being implemented. The headteacher/principal and their deputies may be in a particularly strong position to ensure that any research they undertake leads to the implementation of recommendations. The Principal of St Malachy's College was using the whole range of his assignments and dissertation to investigate different aspects of the school, but all with the intention of changing the culture to one which is collaborative and learning centred. The headteacher of Kents Hill First School, researching the induction of new staff, was 'in an ideal position to implement her research' (Lumby, Chapter 2, p. 28) and carrying out the research helped her to establish herself in her new role as well as ensuring a good start to the career of her NQT.

In analysing the effect of research projects on whole school change, Middlewood in Chapter 8 shows the important part that research can play in 'opening doors' to change and improvement in two cases, one where a positive rather than negative discipline scheme was successfully launched in a secondary school, and the other where homework and the partnership with parents was successfully reviewed. In both cases the culture of the school was receptive to such positive changes and there was awareness that, once implemented, it was important that the changes were monitored and evaluated.

The overt backing of senior management may play an important part in validating the research of others in the eyes of the rest of the school or college. Four of the headteachers in the schools where there were research groups had actually joined the group, although they felt some difficulty about the ambiguity of their membership. As a result, they judged that they learnt more about the research projects being undertaken through being interviewed and through the sharing of results than through membership of the group.

However, the successful outcome of research that has a whole-school or college outcome may be given impetus by the serendipity of events. The decision to investigate a new pay structure at Charles Keene College, reported in Chapter 5, was given fresh impetus by the merger with another college, which required the senior management to consider this very area. The Personnel Manager was able to reflect that the research project added value, in that, although a new pay structure would have to be developed, the research enabled a better scheme to be devised. In many cases, it appears that the impact of research is increased because it is one factor, amongst a range of others that are all leading to change. The Deputy Head of the girls' school, whose research on governors reported in Chapter 5 was largely implemented, stated that her work acted as a 'catalyst' within a situation where change was obviously necessary. In Chapter 5, the two pieces of research that helped to bring about a reassessment of the place of associate staff were both deemed to have informed and speeded a process that was likely to have occurred. In Summerhill the headteacher commented that 'because the research was helpful, useful and could just be implemented, it [the change] actually happened'.

In the case of large-scale changes, the support of others for the research is of great importance. This may occur in terms of doing the research and is most apparent where there is a group working together, as in the schools described by David Middlewood in Chapters 6 to 8. He comments on the universal agreement amongst those interviewed of the importance of this group in providing support and encouragement to each other and also in allowing the individual students, who might otherwise not meet, the opportunity to discuss research issues together. Although the support of the headteacher, principal or senior management is obviously valuable, it is not only such support that counts. In the example of research in Summerhill School (Chapter 5) the support of the associate staff themselves was just as important as the support of the headteacher in leading to the successful implementation of the research findings.

Comments from the questionnaire also stressed the value of support from colleagues in the school or college:

> Good support from teachers, many of whom were also keen to see the results.

> The teachers were usually very willing to participate in the study and had a lot to offer in the way of suggestions as to how to best carry out the survey.

It is particularly noticeable from the survey responses, but also from the case studies, that there is a variation in the ways that teachers and other staff in the schools and colleges respond to the research demands of their colleagues. In most cases it appears that the response is supportive, but this is not always so. The culture of the school is likely to be a major factor that contributes to the degree of support that staff give to research and other efforts intended to lead to improvement. Similarly, the successful implementation of recommendations arising from research will be dependent on the culture of the school or college, and the extent to which the research investigation is allied to the dominant values of that culture.

The Importance of Institutional Culture

The intangible nature of culture makes it hard to define. However, a culture of a school or college may be perceived through the particular presentation of aspects of the school or college such as: the dominant values and beliefs; the shared norms and meaning; the rituals and ceremonies; and the institution's heroes and heroines (Bush, 1998). In addition, the structures of management relationships and meetings may also exemplify a culture. A rigid hierarchy rather than a 'flat' management structure with an emphasis on team work says much about the culture of the institution. A school which has a compulsory uniform, an emphasis on traditions including prize-giving and a display of cups and group photographs in a panelled entrance hall is likely to have a very different culture from one with no uniform, an emphasis on each student reaching their individual potential and an entrance hall featuring a reception desk and a display of indoor plants. However, the culture also includes the way that people respond to one another:

> Organisational culture is the characteristic spirit and belief of an organisation, demonstrated, for example, in the norms and values that are generally held about how people should treat each other, the nature of the working relationships that should be developed and attitudes to change. These norms are deep, taken-for-granted assumptions that are not always expressed, and are often known without being understood.
>
> (Torrington and Weightman, 1993, p. 45)

The investigations into the role of associate staff in Chapter 5 provide excellent examples of the way in which the culture may be subtly changed by research. Staff who were previously defined negatively as 'non-teaching staff' were called 'associate staff,' the research affected attitudes and brought about conceptual change. Similarly, the research on governors reported in Chapter 3 helped to re-define their role and began to change the ways in which the governors were viewed in the school. In the schools reported in Chapter 6, where there were multiple research projects, the effect on relationships was felt in terms of changes in the relationship between staff and students, between members of the teaching staff, but also in helping to integrate part-time and associate staff. Elsewhere, the research on associate staff reported in Chapter 5 also helped to reduce the sense of isolation:

What the research did was to raise awareness among the associate staff of the possibility of change and of the willingness of management to lead that change. It made them feel more involved in the process because they were aware of management being consulted in the planning of the questionnaire.

(Lumby, p. 175)

In the schools where multiple research projects were taking place, the fact that staff of different levels of seniority were working together through the research made all aware of the resulting improvement in understanding and communications. Staff reported seeing each other in 'a new light'.

References have already been made to the variable nature of the responses of staff to requests for information via interviews and questionnaires, this variability being related to the supportive or less supportive nature of the culture. However, the presence of a group of teachers actively involved in researching aspects of the school in the spirit of improvement may in turn affect the culture of the school. In Chapter 7 Middlewood comments on the extent of the involvement of those who were not actively associated with the research. The fact that the group of researchers was disparate meant that they operated in all the areas of the school, ensuring a maximum dissemination of knowledge and interest about the group.

In itemising some of the ways in which improvement is encouraged, Hopkins (1994) stresses that there should be a common understanding of the vision and the main purposes of the institution, and that collaboration amongst staff is vital for both staff development and school improvement. One of the effects of multiple research projects established in Chapter 7 is that those participating had 'widened their understanding of the school as a whole' (Middlewood, p. 114). As a result the teachers felt empowered, able to criticise and were seen to be experiencing more job satisfaction. The headteachers of these schools were aware that the increase in understanding and collaboration as a result of the wide-scale research activity had made their jobs as leaders easier. Beare *et al.* (1993) in listing current generalisations about leadership in education include: 'Vision must be communicated in a way which secures commitment among members of the organisation.' It would seem that the multiple research projects and increased understanding of the research practitioners are helping to do just that.

There is a strong link between the culture and the leadership of the school (Beare *et al.*, 1993) and where the senior management of the school or college is supportive of research, it is likely that the culture of the institution will also be conducive to staff conducting investigations and to the implementation of outcomes. Both David Middlewood and Jacky Lumby have made a case for fruitful research to be linked to the idea of the school and college as learning organisations, where learning occurs at many levels and leads to organisational learning and change.

However, the culture of the school may also work in a way that stultifies the effects of research. The attempt to analyse the current recruitment policy reported in a secondary school in Chapter 2 was unsuccessful, largely because of the nature of the leadership of the school. Structures, such as the pattern of relationships between role holders, and the structure of meetings and committees, are 'the physical manifestation of the culture of the organisation' (Bush, 1998, p. 36). A school which has a bureaucratic, hierarchical structure is unlikely to be affected by the research findings of a teacher who does not have senior responsibility:

> Unfortunately, most of the assignments that I have completed have had very little direct impact on the College. One of the reasons for this, I suspect, is that in hierarchical terms, I am not in a position to follow through any benefits.
> (Questionnaire response)

It is likely that where there is research activity, and where that research activity is welcomed and results implemented, the culture of the institution is one that will be conducive to improvement. Stoll and Fink (1996), building on the work of Hopkins *et al.* (1994), have developed a model of five idealised types of school cultures and identified their relationship to both school improvement and school effectiveness. Moving schools are both effective and improving. Cruising schools, since

	Improving	Declining
Effective	Moving	Cruising
	Strolling	
Ineffective	Struggling	Sinking

(Stoll and Fink, 1996, Figure 6.1, p. 85)

Figure 10.1   Effectiveness and improvement typology of schools

they are effective may be well regarded, but these schools often have a high ability intake and may add little value in the education of their students; they are unlikely to be actively seeking improvement. Strolling schools may be trying to improve, but are doing so slowly, possibly in ways that are not well defined within the school. Struggling schools are ineffective in terms of examination results but trying to improve, whilst sinking schools are both ineffective and deteriorating. They may have been identified as failing schools.

It is likely that many of the schools identified by David Middlewood in Chapters 6 to 8 are schools which could be defined in this typology as 'moving'. In these schools, the movement is likely to be caused by the presence of a significant group of teachers undertaking research and improving their own understanding of the values and vision of the school with a culture and leadership that are supportive of their efforts. However, there were two schools which might be identified as 'struggling', those schools faced either with closure, or with special measures. Here research was being carried out by a relatively large proportion of staff, determined to do their best for their pupils and to maintain their own morale and motivation in difficult circumstances.

In considering the factors that lead to the successful implementation of research findings, the motivation, persistence and hard work of the individual cannot be discounted. Jacky Lumby includes the quality of the research project itself as well as the determination of the researcher as two of the factors that contributed to the success of the research in William Shrewsbury School, reported in Chapter 5. The importance of the individual is also emphasised in the same chapter where a difficult although worthy research project undertaken by the Head of Music on the management of peripatetic staff has not come to fruition through a combination of factors in the school, supplemented by personal difficulties, that prevented the researcher from implementing findings. However, Lumby comments that it may be too early to estimate the true value of this piece of research, since circumstances could change and allow the potential benefits of the recommendations to be felt.

RESEARCH AND THE REFLECTIVE PRACTITIONER

There is no doubt that individuals benefit professionally and personally from undertaking research. All those interviewed and surveyed would testify to the growth in their own knowledge, experience and understanding, both in the areas investigated and in terms of theory and research:

> I have learnt the importance of healthy relations between headteacher and the community.

> Personally I feel that I have been able to make a more effective contribution to the work of the team.

> Very useful increase in knowledge of literature re middle management effectiveness.

> How to do *real* research, and write literature reviews to explore current knowledge: the whole academic process.

A deputy head who carried out an investigation into middle management commented in her questionnaire that:

> By encouraging a structural dialogue as well as reflection it has improved the quality of middle management at the school. It has demonstrated the obvious benefits of making the school a learning organisation for the staff as well as pupils.

In Chapter 6 David Middlewood identifies the benefits to individuals in terms of their own professional development and specifically the appreciation of their own growing skills as researchers. Their stance as reflective practitioners was enhanced by their 'rediscovered' interest in reading relevant academic literature.

The concept of the reflective practitioner is taken further in Chapter 7 where, using the concept of the learning organisation, Middlewood is able to show not only the increase in skills and knowledge of the researchers but also the perception that they had achieved: 'a deeper sense of awareness of learning' (p. 103) and that they were learning together:

> Every single person said that they had found the support of the school group and the opportunity to work with others one of the most valuable and important factors in the success of the research programmes.
>
> (p. 109)

In addition, all those in the school who were not directly involved in doing the research still felt involvement. There was a high level of support, and there was evidence that those who were interviewed were grateful for the opportunity this gave them in turn to reflect on their own practice. One of the deputy principals described the series of interviews in which she participated as being 'refreshing', 'challenging' and 'enlightening' (p. 112).

There is a clear relationship between reflection and the conditions that Hopkins (1994, p.80) identifies as crucial to school improvement. He sees the processes of improvement as being informed by reflection and feedback and specifically mentions teachers working in groups to: 'adapt educational ideas to their own context and professional needs.'

In Chapter 2, Jacky Lumby points out that 'practitioner research supports the process of learning as it is sustained and systematic' (p. 24), but makes the case that in order to meet the criteria of being a 'learning organisation', the research should also have an impact on the organisation in terms of 'conceptual and instrumental change'. The importance of a supportive and collaborative culture in bringing about such change has already been considered. However, in some schools and colleges the culture may be less one of collaboration and more one where micro-political skills are needed in order for changes to occur.

RESEARCH AND MICRO-POLITICS

In one of the schools reported by Middlewood (Chapter 7) the researchers were clear that there were no such things as 'career threatening recommendations, and that the culture allowed: "Healthy two-way debate, positive conflict and disagreement".' However, this is certainly not the case in all schools and colleges. In many cases, collaborative work is not necessarily seen as positive, and heads and principals are not always welcoming of research which suggests and recommends change. This may be particularly true in cultures with a high power-distance ratio (Hofstede, 1980) (see Chapter 9). It may be that in some cases the researcher is running the risk of at least disapproval and at worst dismissal.

In cultural environments such as these it may be particularly useful to develop micro-political skills to find ways of 'infiltrating' the results of the research in instances where a direct presentation is not possible. In the case of the secondary school investigation into recruitment practice, the findings were tempered by the intervention of a senior master rather than being fed directly to the headteacher. The senior master saw possibilities of using the work over time in a diplomatic and indirect way, working within the confines of the existing culture.

The importance of the support of senior managers in achieving the implementation of research recommendations may lead to a conclusion that to be successful a researcher should develop micro-political skills. In Chapter 4, Jacky Lumby relates the relative success of the research undertaken in Loughborough College to the micro-political skills of the researcher who had built support for the changes implicit in the research amongst the lecturing staff. She goes so far as to claim, in the conclusion of Chapter 2, that the researcher might consider choosing their area of research on the basis of the micro-political support that is available to them. Research is more likely to be successful in achieving its purpose when it is in accord with the thinking of powerful people within the organisation. Lumby suggests (Chapter 4, p. 54) that:

> it is the context in which research is undertaken rather than the nature of the research itself, which will ensure that there is an impact at an organisational level.

Certainly the importance of some support for the researcher is emphasised by the experience of a lone researcher in a college, reported in Chapter 3, that:

> the completed assignment received no response, neither from my Head of Faculty, the Head of School (the subject of the enquiry), nor any member of the College's senior management team. (Coleman, p. 41)

It is possible that a research investigation may be annexed by those in a position of power for micro-political reasons. In Chapter 4 recommendations from research that was designed to support the learning of business studies students related to restructuring of roles, and it appeared that the findings were then used to justify restructuring which related to financial considerations. This example highlights the question of research ethics, referred to in the previous chapter.

THE DISSEMINATION OF PRACTITIONER RESEARCH

Immaculately carried out research that is not even read by others in the institution is truly 'an academic exercise'. The anticipation attached to effective research is that the researcher will at least build dissemination of results into their research plan. Johnson (1994, pp. 13–14) states that the researcher 'has a duty to make dissemination possible', and goes on to suggest that:

> the teacher-investigator may find it worthwhile to prepare a short list of key issues arising from his [sic] research which can form the basis of formal or informal discussion with colleagues.

Poor dissemination was also a criticism levelled against professional researchers (Tooley and Darby, 1998). Southworth (1998, p. 21) makes the point that:

> Too much research remains on library shelves, rather than in the minds of practitioners and embodied in their professional actions.

However, the dissemination of the findings of practitioner researchers presents different issues. In most cases researcher practitioners are not looking to disseminate their findings beyond their own institution. Research work intended to lead to institutional improvement usually originates from the identified needs of that particular institution and dissemination may only be the first phase of the implementation or embedding of change.

It is in the nature of practitioner research and of school improvement that the findings are specific to the institution. Indeed, there are reported difficulties in attempting to disseminate the findings of research on school improvement from one group of schools to another:

> The reported research highlighted two areas which are proving to be problematical in trying to make research accessible to practitioners. Firstly, the idea implicit in presenting research is that it provides a model for change. The findings from school effectiveness research are often presented as lists of characteristics common to effective (or in some cases ineffective) schools. In

the case of the former they often take on the role of 'sharing good practice', with the lists of characteristics becoming a model for change. Research that can be easily translated into this form is then offered as being relevant to practice. However, the danger is that the practical issues of 'how to do it' subsumes the 'why to do it' or the appropriateness of doing it at all.

(Wikeley, 1998, pp. 60–61)

The research clearly identified that the simple dissemination of findings from one school to another is not sufficient for there to be any real impact, but there also needs to be reflection on how the research findings might relate to practice:

If improvement initiatives are to be seen as relevant rather than imposed, then dissemination of research, such as that on effective departments, has to be seen as focusing reflection on practice rather than as indicators for improvement.

(*ibid.*, p. 72)

Huberman (1993, p. 47) points out that when researchers hand over a study to a set of practitioners, their low 'permeability to unwelcome findings' usually spell instant oblivion for the study, however valid and well-packaged its findings. However, successful dissemination and implementation may be made possible by 'sustained interactivity'; an ongoing 'conversation' between researchers and practitioners around the import of the study rather than a straightforward extrapolation from the findings to the local setting (*ibid.*, p. 37).

Considering a research partnership between primary schools, a higher education institution and an LEA, Southworth (1998, p. 20) comments that:

'working with' colleagues, rather than 'working on' practitioners, is more productive and ultimately more powerful because the sharing of ideas is so stimulating and challenging.

In terms of the practitioner research outlined in Chapters 2 to 8, dissemination of findings and their application within the institution appear to be dependent on the extent to which the research is in accord with the aims and values of the school or college and its senior management. This was certainly the case in the William Shrewsbury School (Chapter 5) where the headteacher 'was eager to use the work [on associate staff] to contribute towards achieving the guiding vision of the school, where all were valued' (Lumby p. 71). Where there was a significant group of researchers, the impact through dissemination of the findings of research appears to be effective. The schools discussed in Chapter 7 had effected a level of cultural change through the process of research and amongst the factors identified as important in this process were the 'careful and continuous presentation of the research group's work to the rest of the staff' (Middlewood, p. 118).

In schools where researchers are working alone and do not have the particular support of the senior management team it is harder to disseminate findings and thus for those findings to have an impact. Middlewood (Chapter 8, p. 135) points out that the impact of the work of a single teacher 'may be unduly dependent upon personal status or because the work coincided with the mood of need of the time'. However, dissemination could also be achieved through micro-political activity and the effective sponsorship of the research by a member of the senior management team as appeared to be the case in Rugby College (Chapter 4). It could also depend on circumstances as in the case of Charles Keene College (Chapter 5). However, the work of either a single teacher or of a group of researchers is more likely to be implemented where the research has the backing of senior managers and the topic of research is seen to be relevant to the needs of the school or college.

A RESEARCHER PRACTITIONER PARADIGM

In considering the nature of practitioner research, the question arises of its relationship to existing paradigms, and the extent to which practitioner research may actually represent a separate, identifiable research paradigm.

Southworth (1998) argues for the principle of 'inclusiveness' in research in education, allowing for the interplay of the different research approaches as appropriate. He sees inclusiveness as relating to the use of:

> both quantitative and qualitative methods. The so-called paradigm wars in social science have led to numerous casualties, not least of which is continuation of polarised thinking. Either/or thinking has no place in our post-modern world.
>
> (p. 20)

As we have seen in Chapter 1, the apparent conflicts between positivist and relativist or interpretive paradigms of research are generally resolved in practice.

Possibly the most important question to ask about practitioner research is 'what is its purpose?' There can be no single answer to this, since, although practitioner research is closely identified with school and college improvement, the impact on the organisation is not the only outcome. As has been seen from the research investigations reported earlier in this book, there can be considerable benefit for the individual researcher in terms of the growth of their own knowledge, skills and understanding. Although the effects on the institution and the individual can be separately assessed, it is also possible that the impact on the individual may have an unpredictable longer term effect on the institution. Later evaluation would have to take place in order to estimate the extent to which this might occur.

Despite the importance of the impact on the individual researcher, most research undertaken in schools and colleges is intended to promote improvement. The links between practitioner research reported here and elsewhere and institutional improvement are strong. The 'doors' to school improvement (Joyce, 1991) can all be seen to be related to practitioner research: studying research findings; the collection of site-specific information; introducing changes in the curriculum and elsewhere; groups of teachers studying together. All of this in conditions of collegiality fostering the development of professional relations.

If practitioner research is closely identified with institutional improvement and change there is an undeniable link with action research. The six stages of research identified by Middlewood in Chapter 8, that were intended to change a negative to a positive student ethos, have a parallel with the action research spiral and the eight stages of action research (Bassey, 1998b) shown in Chapter 1. To the extent that action research makes use of empirical methods and is associated with practitioners instituting change, action research is likely to be incorporated into the paradigm of the researcher practitioner. However:

> Despite the proliferation of action research projects in recent years, many tensions remain between different understandings of what action research actually involves, and what it can and ought to claim on behalf of understanding and action.
>
> (Bryant, 1996, p. 108)

A strength of practitioner research must lie in the nature of the understanding of those carrying out the research. Despite questions being raised about the ability of teachers to carry out research (Hillage *et al.*, 1998; Tooley and Darby, 1998), a strong case is made for the involvement of practitioners in educational research (Hargreaves, 1996; Southworth, 1998). The unique contribution of practitioners to research is summed up thus:

> For those who see the possibilities of learning from teacher researchers, it is precisely their inside perspectives as participants and the distinctive lenses they use to make sense of classroom life over long periods of time that promise to illuminate new aspects of teaching, learning and schooling. The debate here is not ... one of generalizability and truth, on the one hand, versus context-specific and biased information on the other. Rather the debate is related to larger questions about the kinds, forms, and perspectives on knowledge that will ultimately help to improve educational practice.
>
> (Cochran-Smith and Lytle, 1998, p. 26)

If improvement of educational practice is to be achieved, the research itself must be disseminated and embedded in the practice of the educational institution. As we have seen above, this will be hindered or helped by the culture of the organisation and practitioners may need to be aware of aspects of their institutional culture and of its micro-political dimensions. In addition, individual practitioner researchers will need to exhibit a great deal of determination, even in supportive cultures, in order to ensure that their research findings and recommendations are implemented to support change.

> The relationship between data, theory and action in teachers action research is, thus, more complex than one might at first suppose. Theory from data alone will not automatically tell the teacher action researcher how to act, or how to apply and implement her research. However internally valid the research epistemology may be, it may not adequately account for the extraneous circumstances in the research environment that can make or break effective application ... But the institution too, will have a biography, a history and ecology of its own that the wise teacher action researcher, as change agent, will try to account for as she seeks to link data to action.
>
> (Dadds, 1995, p. 142)

The role of the practitioner researcher is eclectic, combining knowledge and theory of both education and research within the context of their specialised knowledge of practice and exhibiting both determination to bring about change and a sensitive awareness of the conditions most likely to support improvement.

REFERENCES

Adler, S., Laney, J. and Packer M. (1993). *Managing Women: Feminism and Power in Educational Management*. Buckingham, Open University Press.

Ainscow, M., Hopkins, D., Southworth, G. and West, M. (1994). *Creating the Conditions for School Improvement*. London: David Fulton.

Al Khalifa, E. (1992). 'Management by halves: women teachers and school management'. In N. Bennett, M. Crawford and C. Riches (Eds.), *Managing Change in Education: Individual and organizational perspectives*. London: Paul Chapman Publishing.

Argyris, C. and Schon, D. (1981). *Organisational Learning* (2nd edition). Reading, Mass: Addison-Wesley.

Aspinwall, K. and Pedlar, M. (1997). Schools as learning organisations. In B. Fidler, S. Russell and T. Simkins (Eds.), *Choices for Self-Managing Schools*. London: Paul Chapman.

Bangs, J. (1996). Why Homework? *The Teacher*. November. London: National Union of Teachers.

Bassey, M. (1998a). Enhancing teaching through research. In *Professional Development Today, Vol. 1, Issue 2*, April, 39–46.

Bassey, M. (1998b). Action research for improving educational practice. In R. Halsall (Ed.), *Teacher Research and School Improvement: Opening doors from the inside*. Buckingham: Open University Press.

Beare, H., Caldwell, B. and Millikan, R. (1993). Leadership. In M. Preedy (Ed.), *Managing the Effective School*. London: Paul Chapman Publishing.

Bell, J. (1987). *Doing Your Research Project*. Milton Keynes: Open University Press.

Bennett, N. (1995). *Managing Professional Teachers: Middle management in primary and secondary schools*. London: Paul Chapman.

Bloom, B. (Ed.) (1956). *Taxonomy of Educational Objectives*. New York: McKay.

Bogden, R. and Biklen, S. (1992). *Qualitative Research for Education: An Introduction to Theory and Methods*. London: Allyn & Bacon.

Bolam, R., McMahon, A., Pocklington, K. and Weindling, D. (1993). *Effective Management in Schools*. London: HMSO.

Bollen, R. (1996). School effectiveness and school improvement. In D. Reynolds, R. Bollen, B. Creemers, D. Hopkins, L. Stoll and N. Lagerweij. *Making Good Schools: Linking school effectiveness and school improvement*. London: Routledge.

Brain, G. (1994). Reward systems and management. In G. Brain (Ed.), *Managing and Developing People*. Blagdon: The Staff College, in association with the Association for Colleges.

Bryant, I. (1996). Action research and reflective practice. In D. Scott, and R. Usher (Eds.), *Understanding Educational Research*. London: Routledge.

Bush, T. (1995). *Theories of Educational Management* (2nd edition). London: Paul Chapman.

Bush, T. (1997). The changing context of management in education. In T. Bush and D. Middlewood, *Managing People in Education*. London: Paul Chapman.

Bush, T. (1998). Organisational culture and strategic management. In D. Middlewood and J. Lumby (Eds.), *Strategic Management in Schools and Colleges*. London: Paul Chapman.

Bush, T. and Middlewood, D. (1997). *Managing People in Education*. London: Paul Chapman Publishing.

Carter, K. and Halsall, R. (1998). Teacher research for school improvement. In R. Halsall (Ed.), *Teacher Research and School Improvement: Opening doors from the inside*. Buckingham: Open University Press.

Chan, D. and Hui, E. (1995). Burnout and coping among Chinese secondary school teachers in Hong Kong. In *British Journal of Educational Psychology, Vol. 65*, 15–25.

Cochran-Smith, M. and Lytle, S. L. (1998). Teacher research: The question that persists. In *International Journal of Leadership in Education: Theory and practice, Vol. 1, No. 1*, 19–36.

Cohen, L. and Manion, L. (1994). *Research Methods in Education* (4th edition). London: Routledge.

Coleman, M. (1994). Women in educational management. In T. Bush and J. West-Burnham (Eds.), *The Principles of Educational Management*. Harlow: Longman.

Coleman, M. (1996). The management style of female headteachers. In *Educational Management and Administration, Vol. 24, No. 2*, 163–174.

Coleman, P. (1998). *Parent, Student and Teacher Collaboration: The power of 3*. London: Paul Chapman Publications.

Corno, L. (1996). Homework is a complicated thing. In *Educational Researcher, Vol. 25, No. 8*, 27–30.

Covey, P. (1989). *The Seven Habits of Highly Effective People*. New York: Simon and Schuster.

Creemers, B. (1994). *The Effective School*. London: Cassell.

Creemers, B. and Reezigt, G. (1997). School effectiveness and school improvement: Sustaining links. In *School Effectiveness and School Improvement, Vol. 8, No. 4*, 396–429.

Dadds, M. (1995). *Passionate Inquiry and School Development*. London: Falmer.

Davidson, M. (1997). *The Black and Ethnic Woman Manager*. London: Paul Chapman.

Davies, B. (1997). Reengineering and restructuring education – Introduction. In *School Leadership and Management, Vol. 17, No. 2*, 173–185.

Day, C. (1996). Leadership and professional development: Developing reflective practice. In H. Busher and R. Saran (Eds.), *Managing Teachers as Professionals in Schools*. London: Kogan Page.

Deal, T. (1985). The symbolism of effective schools. In *Elementary School Journal, Vol. 85, No. 5*, 605–620.

DFEE (1997), *Statistics of Education Teachers in England and Wales 1997*. London: Government Statistical Service.

Dimmock, C. (1998). Restructuring Hong Kong's schools: The applicablity of Western theories, policies and practices to an Asian culture. In *Educational Management and Administration, Vol. 26, No. 4*, 363–377.

Earley, P. (1994). *Lecturers' Workload and Factors Affecting Stress Levels*. Windsor: NFER.

Easterby-Smith, M., Thorpe, R. and Lowe, A. (1994). The philosophy of research design. In N. Bennett, R. Glatter and R. Levacic (Eds.), *Improving Educational Management through Research and Consultancy*. London: Paul Chapman.

Ebbutt, D. (1985). Educational action research: Some general concerns and specific quibbles. In R. G. Burgess (Ed.), *Issues in Qualitative Research: Qualitative methods*. Lewes: Falmer.

Edwards, R. (1997). *Changing Places? Flexibility, lifelong learning and a learning society*. London: Routledge.

Elliott, J. (1991). *Action Research for Educational Change*. Milton Keynes: Open University Press.

Ferrario, M. (1994). Women as managerial leaders. In M. J. Davidson and R. J. Burke (Eds.), *Women in Management: Current research issues*. London: Paul Chapman Publishing.

Fullan, M. (1985). Change processes and strategies at the local level. *The Elementary School Journal, Vol. 85, No. 3,* 391–421.

Fullan, M. (1994). *Change Forces*. London: Falmer.

Fullan, M. and Hargreaves, A. (1992). *What's Worth Fighting for in your School*. Buckingham: Open University Press.

Further Education Development Agency (1995). *Mapping the FE Sector*. London: DfEE.

Garratt, B. (Revised edition 1994). *The Learning Organisation*. London: Harper Collins.

Gartside, P., Allan, J. and Munn, P. (1988). *In at the Deep End? Induction at Colleges of Further Education*. Edinburgh: SCRE.

Glatter, R. (1988). The management of school improvement. In R. Glatter, M. Preedy, C. Riches and M. Masterton (Eds.), *Understanding School Management*. Milton Keynes: Open University Press.

Gray, H. L. (1993). Gender issues in management training. In J. Ozga (Ed.), *Women in Educational Management*. Buckingham: Open University Press.

Gray, J. (1998). *The Contribution of Educational Research to the Cause of School Improvement: A professorial lecture*. London University: Institute of Education.

Habermas, J. (1972). *Knowledge and Human Interests*. London: Heinemann.

Hall, V. (1997). Management roles in education. In T. Bush and D. Middlewood (Eds.), *Managing People in Education*. London: Paul Chapman.

Harber, C. and Davies, L. (1998). *School Management and Effectiveness in Developing Countries: The post-bureaucratic school*. London: Cassell.

Hargreaves, D. (1996). Teaching as a research-based profession: Possibilities and prospects. *The Teacher Training Agency Annual Lecture*. London: TTA.

Hargreaves, D. (1997). A road to the learning society. In *School Leadership and Management, Vol. 17, No. 1,* 9–21.

Hargreaves, D. (1998). Improving research to enhance teaching. In *Professional Development Today*, Vol. 1, Issue 2, 47–55.

Hegarty, S. (1998). Orchard with too little fruit. *The Guardian,* 28/7/98, 21.

Hillage, J., Pearson, R., Anderson, A., Tamkin, P. (1998). *Excellence in Research on Schools, Research Report No. 74,* London: DfEE.

HMI (Wales) (1985) *Schools in Action*. Welsh Office.

Hofstede, G. (1980). *Culture's Consequences: International differences in work-related values*. Beverly Hills: Sage.

Holland, G. (1998). Learning in the twenty first century. In *New Childhood, Vol. 13, Issue 1, Spring*. National Association for Primary Education.

Honey, P. (1991). The learning organisation simplified. In *Training and Development*, July, 30–33.

Hopkins, D. (1994). School improvement in an ERA of change. In P. Ribbins and E. Burridge (Eds.), *Improving Education: Promoting Quality in Schools*. London: Cassell.

Hopkins, D., Ainscow, M. and West, M. (1994). *School Improvement in an Era of Change*. London: Cassell.

Hopkins, D. and Lagerweij, N. (1996). The school improvement knowledge base. In D. Reynolds, R. Bollen, B. Creemers, D. Hopkins, L. Stoll and N. Lagerweij, *Managing Good Schools*. London: Routledge.

Hoyle, E. and McCormick, R. (1976). *Innovation and the Teacher*. Milton Keynes:

Open University Press.

Huberman, M. (1993). Changing minds: The dissemination of research and its effects on practice and theory. In C. Day, J. Calderhead and P. Denicolo (Eds.), *Research on Teacher Thinking*. London: Falmer.

Johnson, D. (1994). *Research Methods in Educational Management*. Harlow: Longman.

Joyce, B. R. (1991). The doors to school improvement, *Educational Leadership, Vol. 48, No. 8*, 59–62.

Kedney, B. and Brownlow, S. (1994). Funding flexibility, *Mendip Paper, 062*. Blagdon: The Staff College.

Kennedy, M. M. (1997). The connection between research and practice. In *Educational Researcher, Vol. 26, No. 7*, 4–12.

Locke, M. (1990). Methodological reflections. In R. Saran and V. Trafford (Eds.), *Research in Education Management and Policy: Retrospect and policy*. London: Falmer.

Lofthouse, M. (1994). Managing learning. In T. Bush and J. West-Burnham (Eds.), *Principles of Educational Management*. Harlow: Longmans.

Lumby, J. (1997a). The learning organisation. In T. Bush and D. Middlewood (Eds.), *Managing People in Education*. London: Paul Chapman.

Lumby, J. (1997b). Developing managers in further education, part two: The process of development. In *Journal of Further and Higher Education, Vol. 21, No. 3*, 367–375.

MacBeath, J. (1998). I didn't know he was ill: The role and value of the critical friend. In L. Stoll and K. Myers (Eds.), *No Quick Fixes: Perspectives on schools in difficulty*. London: Falmer Press.

Marsh, C., (1992). *Key Concepts in Understanding the Curriculum*. London: Falmer Press.

Maw, J. (1977). Defining roles in senior and middle management in secondary schools. In A. Jennings (Ed.), *Management and Headship in the Secondary School*. London: Ward Lock.

Mayo, E. (1933). *The Human Problems of an Industrial Civilisation*. Boston: Harvard Business School.

Middlewood, D. (1997). Managing staff development. In T. Bush and D. Middlewood (Eds.), *Managing People in Education*. London: Paul Chapman.

Middlewood, D. and Parker, R. (1998). Staff development for school improvement. In *Professional Development Today, Vol. 1, Issue 3*, 51–55.

Miles, M. (1986). *Research Findings on the Stages of School Improvement*. New York: Center for Policy Research.

Miles, M. B. and Ekholm, M. (1985). What is school improvement? In W. G. Van Velzen, M. B. Miles, N. Ekholm, U. Hameyer and D. Robin (1985), *Making School Improvement Work*. Leuven, Belgium: Acco Pub.

Miles, M. B. and Huberman, A. M. (1994). *Qualitative Data Analysis*. London: Sage Publications Ltd.

Morgan, G. (1986). *Images of Organization*. London: Sage.

Morgan, G. (1989). Empowering human resources. In C. Riches and C. Morgan (Eds.), *Human Resource Management In Education*. Milton Keynes: Open University Press.

Mortimore, P. and Mortimore, J. with Thomas, H. (1994). *Managing Associate Staff: Innovation in primary and secondary schools*. London: Paul Chapman.

O'Neill, J. (1994a). Organizational structures and culture. In T. Bush and J. West-Burnham (Eds.), *Principles of Educational Management*. Harlow: Longman.

O'Neill, J. (1994b). Managing human resources. In T. Bush and J. West-Burnham (Eds.), *The Principles of Educational Management*. Harlow: Longman.

Punch, K. and Tuettmann, E. (1990). Correlates of psychological distress among secondary school teachers. In *British Educational Research Journal, Vol. 16, No. 4*, 369–382.

Purvis, J. (1985). Reflections upon doing historical documentary research from a feminist perspective. In R. Burgess, *Strategies of Educational Research: Qualitative methods*. London: The Falmer Press.

Reynolds, D., Sammons, P., Stoll, L., Barber, M. and Hillman, J. (1993). School effectiveness and school improvement in the United Kingdom. In *School Effectiveness and School Improvement, Vol. 7, No. 2*, 135–158.

Ribbins, P. (1988). The role of the middle manager in the secondary school. In R. Glatter, M. Preedy, C. Riches and M. Masterton (Eds.), *Understanding School Management*. Milton Keynes: Open University Press.

Robson, C. (1993). *Real World Research*. Oxford: Blackwell.

Ross, K. N. and Mahlck, L. (Eds.) (1990). *Planning the Quality of Education the Collection and Use of Data for Informed Decision-Making*. Unesco: International Institute for Educational Planning: Pergamon Press.

Sammons, P., Hillman, J. and Mortimore, P. (1995). Key Characterisation of Effective Schools: A review of school effectiveness research. A report by the Institute of Education for the Office for Standards in Education. Institute of Education, University of London.

Schein, V. E. (1994). Managerial sex typing: A persistent and pervasive barrier to women's opportunities. In M. Davidson and R. Burke (Eds.), *Women in Management: Current research issues*. London: Paul Chapman.

Schon, D. A. (1984). Leadership as reflection-in-action. In T. Sergiovanni and J. Corbally (Eds.) *Leadership and Organizational Culture*. Urbana and Chicago: University of Illinois Press.

School Management Task Force (1990). *School Management, The way forward*. London: HMSO.

Seidman, I. E. (1991). *Interviewing as Qualitative Research: A guide for researchers in education and the social sciences*. New York: Teachers College, Columbia University.

Senge, P. (1990). *The Fifth Discipline*. London: Doubleday.

Senge, P. (1991). The learning organisation made plain. In *Training and Development*, October, 37–64.

Shakeshaft, C. (1989). *Women in Educational Administration*. Newbury Park: Sage.

Southworth, G. (1998). Improving educational research: Ways forward through partnership and development. Paper presented at the BERA Annual Conference Symposium on Educational Research – New Directions, August.

Stoll, L. and Fink, D. (1996). *Changing our Schools: Linking school effectiveness and school improvement*. Buckingham: Open University Press.

Stoll, L. and Myers, K. (1998). *No Quick Fixes: Perspectives on schools in difficulty*. London: Falmer Press.

Strachan, J. (1993). Including the personal and the professional: Researching women in educational leadership. In *Gender and Education, Vol. 5, No. 1*, 71–80.

Tasker, M. and Packham, D. (1998). How to publish and be dammed. In *The Independent*, 8/10/98, 4–5.

Teacher Training Agency (1999). *Off the Shelf: MA and PhD dissemination*. London: T.T.A.

Terrell, I., Clinton, B. and Sheraton, K. (1998). Giving learning back to teachers. In *Professional Development Today, Vol. 1, Issue 2*, 13–22.

Thomas, H. and Martin, J. (1996). *Managing Resources for School Improvement*. London: Routledge.

Thompson, M. (1992). Appraisal and equal opportunities. In N. Bennett, M. Crawford and C. Riches (Eds.), *Managing Change in Education: Individual and organizational perspectives*. London: Paul Chapman Publishing.

Tooley, J. and Darby, D. (1998). *Educational Research: A critique*. London: OFSTED.

Torrington, D. and Weightman, J. (1993). The culture and ethos of the school. In M. Preedy (Ed.), *Managing the Effective School*. London: Paul Chapman.

Townsend, R. (1971). *Up the Organisation*. London: Fontana Books.

Travers, C. and Cooper, C. (1996). *Teachers Under Pressure*. London: Routledge.

Trethowan, D. and Smith, D. (1984). *Induction*. London: The Industrial Society.

Usher, R. (1996). Critique of the neglected epistemological assumptions of educational research. In D. Scott and R. Usher (Eds.), *Understanding Educational Research*. London: Routledge.

Verma, S. (1998). *Women Teachers' Perceptions of Careers: Is the glass ceiling relevant?* Unpublished MBA thesis: University of Leicester.

Vulliamy, G., Lewin, K. and Stephens, D. (1990). *Doing Educational Research in Developing Countries: Qualitative strategies*. London: The Falmer Press.

Wagner, J. (1997). The unavoidable intervention of educational research: A framework for reconsidering researcher-practitioner co-operation. In *Educational Researcher, Vol. 26, No. 7*, 13–22.

Wagstaff, J. (1994). HRM in the next decade – an external perspective. In G. Brain (Ed.), *Managing and Developing People*. Bristol: The Staff College and the Association for Colleges.

Waters, M. (1998). Personal development for teachers: Part I. In *Professional Development Today, Vol. 1, Issue 2*, 29–38.

Wikeley, F. (1998). Dissemination of research as a tool for school improvement? In *School Leadership and Management, Vol. 18, No. 1*, 59–73.

Williams, G. L. (1984). Observing and recording meetings. In J. Bell,, T. Bush, A. Fox, J. Goodey and S. Goulding (Eds.), *Conducting Small-Scale Investigations in Educational Management*. London: Harper and Row.

Wise, C. (1997). The role of the academic middle manager in secondary schools. Paper given at the BERA conference, Sept.

AUTHOR INDEX

178

SUBJECT INDEX

DATE DUE

GAYLORD   #3522PI   Printed in USA